Haunts

MW01222441

By David Wolfe

© 2016

Pen It! Publications, LLC

ISBN #:   978-1539386827

ISBN #:   1539386821

Edited by: Pen It! Publications, LLC

Cover Art by: Debi Stanton

First Edition © 2016

www.hauntsofowensboro.com

Pen It! Publications, LLC
penitpublications@yahoo.com
www.penitpublications.com
www.BuyMeBooksNow.com

Acknowledgements

I would like to thank Joe Ford, William (Todd) Reynolds, Ron Mayhew, the staff of the Owensboro Public Library, members of Downtown Owensboro, Belinda Thomson and give special notice to the book *Sixty Years of Owensboro* for helping me with my research and for their assistance with my ghostly tours.

I would especially like to thank my family for their support; my grandparents, my parents, and my wife and children.

Thank you!

Pen It! Publications, LLC

Preface

Many people throughout the years have asked me how I became interested in ghosts, Bigfoot, UFOs, and all things paranormal. I guess I would have to say a couple of different personal experiences helped build my interest in the subjects.

I was born in Coshocton, Ohio on September 8, 1971 and I lived in a home that was 100 years old. While living in this house with parents, we never seemed to have any paranormal activity. However, after my dad and mom divorced, it was just my mom and I alone... that's when things began to happen.

I was about six-year-old, when I saw my first ghostly apparition. During a two-year span, from age four to six years old, weird things would happen at the house. My mom also had ghostly experiences, but I'll save all these stories for another book. I will say that the ghostly apparition I saw brought out the curiosity in me. From that time on, I was intrigued with ghosts. I wanted to know what they were, where they came from, why they were here in my house, and why they were stuck on Earth.

My family has also been a big influence in my interest in ghost stories. Grandma and Grandpa McFarland are from Eastern Kentucky and are some of the best ghost story tellers I have ever known.

Grandpa would tell us stories, around the holidays, about the Wildman of Eastern Kentucky (Bigfoot) and other oddities. As children, we would gather around him with wide eyes, eager to hear the tales.

My Grandma was a great storyteller and knew even more stories than my grandpa. She would tell stories about the headless man, who walked down the railroad tracks. She also told a story about being a child and witnessing an old prospector with a mule who vanished, right before her eyes.

There were many stories about ghostly apparitions and premonitions and many other ghostly tales. I was so intrigued with my grandparents' stories that I would hang on every word. I would make them tell the stories over and over again, even though they had already told them a million times. I devoured every word, I couldn't get enough.

My Uncle Terry was another family member who would chime in after Grandma or Grandpa would tell their tales. His stories were scary, but they were also funny. I often think about my grandparents and their childhood back in Kentucky. They lived back before cable, HBO, and the internet. They had music and good ghost stories for entertainment. What a time that must have been.

My mom was a good storyteller, in her own right. She would tell ghost stories of the house we used to live in on Chestnut Hill in Coshocton, Ohio. This was the same house where I saw my first apparition.

My dad shared stories about Bigfoot and how he saw an apparition, at the same age as I was when I saw my first apparition. Dad loved to tell stories, mainly about Bigfoot. He loved to tell about his days of hunting and hearing a big creature following him. He would say that he knew wasn't a deer.

My family had a great influence on me and my interest in the paranormal. My dad would always tease me about writing a book of ghost stories. He would call and ask me, "You wrote that book yet?" Well, Dad, I finally did it.

The person who I have to give credit to who influenced me the most is Joe Ford. I moved to Owensboro, Kentucky when I was in 6th grade and had just barely turned 13. Ford, came to Burns Middle School to speak. I listened to him and his stories reminded me of my grandparent's stories.

He would always come around Halloween and he would weave tales about haunted Owensboro and other scary places. After he was done, I would say to myself, "I want to do that. That's what I want to do for a living when I grow up!"

Mr. Ford probably didn't realize how much of an enormous influence he was on me. As a kid, I probably bugged him all the time by going into the museum and asking him questions about ghosts, Bigfoot, and some of the cool pets that he had. He had a boa constrictor and a pet tarantula, which I would never touch, because I was too afraid.

As I grew older we became pretty good friends and I followed him all the way to Brescia University, where I went to college. I sat enthralled as I listened to each and every story he told me. He shared stories about the history of the town, ghost stories, and even Bigfoot stories. I listened in amazement, head in hand, elbows on a desk, and practically drooling at every word he said. I miss him dearly and I keep in contact with his wife, quite often.

Grace, Mr. Ford's wife was another great influence on me. I had the desire to take up the mantle of telling ghost stories, where her husband left off. Now I'm telling people ghost stories, but in my own way.

I opened my own ghost tours. In fact, before starting these ghost tours I asked Mr. Ford what he thought, and asked for his blessing. He told me, "If I was a little bit younger I would have done it myself." He told me that it was a great idea because I'm incorporating stories about the history of our beautiful city. Thank you, Mr. Ford, for being a great influence on my life.

There are others who influenced me throughout our great city. Mrs. Belinda Thomson is one of them. When I was preparing to start my tours 11 years ago, I told Mrs. Thomson that I was going to invite the mayor and all these big wigs to a tour. She said, "Wait and let me go out on the tour first and critique you." So, from that time on, she took me under her wing and even shared some of her own ghost stories with me. She is also my acting coach and a person who I hold dear to my heart. She watches out for me and has always been a great shoulder to lean on.

Those many years ago, Mrs. Thomson told me to seek out another friend whose name is Todd Reynolds. You'll hear about him later in the book because he also gave me some great stories. We've worked together, occasionally throughout the years together on other projects and share good stories together when we have the time.

Those are the influences I have had throughout my life. My hope is that you see how, through these influences, I have become the man I am.

I am also a historical actor, tour owner/operator, and substitute teacher for Daviess County Public Schools. I love all these jobs.

My final inspiration is my wife and kids. I guess I write these stories for them too. It's something like a memoir for them to remember me by. My words will last forever. In a way, I can leave them my haunts in words. So, to Kathie, David, and Makenzie, I love you with all my heart.

Note: All these establishment and homes are privately owned. Any trespassing without permission will be prosecuted. I again give thanks to all the owners for their stories and corporation.

Chapter 1

River Front Ghost and Hangings

The Beginning

All good ghost stories have a beginning. Mine starts right at the riverfront where the new Hampton Inn meets Smothers Park. It is here that William Smeathers made his home in 1797. According to *the find a grave website,* Mr. Smeathers committed the very first murder, on those banks of Owensboro, which were called Yellowbanks, at the time, in 1809.

It is said that he was defending his sister's honor against, what I call, ruffians. One of the fellows made advances toward his sister and in self-defense, he killed this ruffian.

I find it creepy that where the park is today, is where the very first murder took place. Who knows if this murderer, long since departed is still lurking around in the park. According to the website https://tshaonline.org/handbook/online/articles/fsm55 the gentleman who was murdered was named Andrew Norris.

Mr. Smeathers was found innocent during the trial, but was told to leave town, just in case Mr. Norris's friends came after him.

It must be noted that Joseph Hamilton Daviess was Mr. Smeathers Attorney. Daviess County, where

Owensboro is, was named after him. As a side note, according to www.findagrave.com, Bill Smeather's wife, Mary, is buried in what is now the parking lot of the Hampton Inn, I also find this somewhat creepy!

So, now, we have a site of a murder and an unmarked grave. Already death in this little town is starting to add up and so are the ghosts.

The Hanging

In the same area, on August 14, 1936, the last public hanging in America took place. The gentleman's name was Rainy Bethea and he was charged with a horrendous crime that took place on 5th and Crittenden Streets in June of that same year. The crime was the rape and murder of Mrs. Lischia Edwards.

A Miss Thomson was supposed to conduct the hanging, since she was the county sheriff. At the time this was very odd and I don't know of anywhere in America that had a female sheriff in 1936. It turns out that Sheriff Thomson did not have to perform the hanging. That task fell to Mr. Hannah and Mr. Hash.

At 5:30 on the morning of August 14, 1936, Mr. Bethea was walked up to the scaffold by Mr. Hannah and Mr. Hash. Here's where my search for facts gets very odd. Mr. Bethea stopped at the first step, took off his shoes and then he pulled out a pair of very girly type socks. He put on the socks and proceeded to walk up the steps. I was very curious about this story, so I went to Mr. Joe Ford to obtain an explanation. I asked him, as we were casually sitting together, "What is the deal with these white socks? Why do I keep coming across them in my research?"

Mr. Ford's response was to mischievously ask, "Do you really want to know?"

I replied, "Yes! Please!!"

Joe told me that the socks were just a rumor. The white socks that Mr. Bethea put on that day were supposedly taken from his victim. These socks were a token for him to remember her by, which is what some serial killers do. While I'm not saying that he was a serial killer, I will say it was rather odd and quite morbid.

Mr. Bethea was standing on the scaffold and Mr. Hannah and Mr. Hash were standing with him. Mr. Hannah had his hands on the noose and Mr. Hash had his hands on the lever. Mr. Hannah put the noose around Mr. Bethea's neck. Everything was quiet throughout the crowd. No one said a word. There is not a peep in the crowd.

Over 15,000 people had camped out for three days to watch this morbid spectacle. Some say it was almost like a macabre circus; there were vendors selling drinks and trinkets. The media had gotten wind that Miss Thomson was going to do the hanging. It is said that reporters came from hundreds of miles away to write the story. Again, she did not have to perform the hanging, so they were disappointed. That job fell to Mr. Hannah and Mr. Hash.

The noose was tightened and ready to go. Mr. Hannah said to Mr. Hash, "Do it!"

Nothing happened.

Again, Mr. Hannah gave the command, "I said, do it!"

Again Mr. Hash ignored the order. It seemed that Mr. Hash was quite drunk that morning.

Mr. Hannah give the command for the third time. "I said do it, now! You're embarrassing me!"

In order for the hanging to be completed, a deputy, who was standing behind Mr. Hash had to assist, by placing Mr. Hash's hand on the lever. Finally, Mr. Bethea fell, swinging between Heaven and Earth.

The media had concocted a plan to further sensationalize the hanging. They concocted a story that the citizens of Owensboro rushed the body and tore it limb from limb. This is a horrible fabrication, for that never took place. In fact, the body hung before the crowd for approximately about 10 minutes.

Today, Mr. Bethea is buried in Potter's Field, in an unmarked grave, in Elmwood Cemetery.

I was curious as to just what happened to those gallows. I asked Mr. Ford, "What happened to the gallows? I would like to see them."

You see, Mr. Ford used to work at the old museum which was located at the corner of 9th and Frederica Streets, where the art museum is located today.

He looked at me when I asked this question and answered, "Yes, I remember what happened to those gallows."

However, he didn't give me the location.

Again, I asked him if I could see the wood from

the gallows. He told me that that legend is they took them down from their location at 9th and Frederica and turned them into beds. So, if you're sleeping on an old bed from the 1930's and you feel a good jar in the middle of the night, it just may be the ghost of Mr. Bethea still hanging around.

According to Keith Lawrence of *The Messenger-Inquirer*, Mr. Bethea wasn't the only person hanged in that area. Although he didn't go into detail, he did say that other hangings took place in that same area.

The parking lot where the Hampton Inn is today once housed an old jail. So, it seems that there was a lot of death in that area.

Mr. Bethea going to the Gallows on August 14th 1936.
http://murderpedia.org/male.B/b/bethea-rainey-photos.htm

Pen It! Publications, LLC

Last public hanging August 14th, 1936.
http://murderpedia.org/male.B/b/bethea-rainey-photos.htm

This ghost story about that area, and is a personal one. Initially, my ghost tours started out of the Crème Coffee House on 2nd Street. Later, we will get to the hauntings that took place there.

At the time, I lead my tours down 2nd Street and turned onto St. Elizabeth Street, where I always told the story of the last public hanging in America, just as I told you. It was around 2008, and there was nothing really in that area at the time.

I'm sharing my story to the tour participants and a lady stepped out in the middle of the street to take a picture. I heard her say, "Oh! My gosh! What is that?"

The crowd of about 30 people all gathered around her in the middle of the street. Right where the hanging had taken place, was a stand-alone, shadowy figure. She was able to capture the figure with the camera on her phone. She took a couple more pictures in the same place and got nothing. We were all shocked because we had just seen the figure.

When people ask me what to do when taking pictures of ghosts, I always tell them take about two or three pictures in the same spot. If something was to appear in the first film and not the second or third, then you just might have captured yourself a ghost.

We were all shocked at this picture. I also have a picture with two forms standing side-by-side. I've often wondered if this was Mr. Hannah and Mr. Hash. It would not surprise me with all the deaths that area has seen. Do the dead still walk around that area?

Pen It! Publications, LLC

Chapter 2

The Big E Ghost

Matilda

The Hampton Inn and Convention Center now stand has a lot of ghost stories.

Let's begin with the area currently occupied by the Convention Center. From 1896 to1939, this area was known as the *Red Light District*. It was notoriously known for the ladies of the night who worked that area of town. There is a story that one of these ladies of the night who lived in a house where the Hampton Inn stands today.

This lady, we will call her Matilda, was going to be married and she was excited about her upcoming wedding day. She was finally going to leave the horrible life style she had been living. The wedding day came and she showed up at the church in her beautiful wedding gown. It was to be a very small wedding, however, there was one problem. Matilda was there, the priest was there, but something to the right of her was missing, the Groom! He left her standing at the alter on her on her wedding night.

Poor Matilda was so distraught over this that she ran back to the only place that would give her refuge, the house of prostitution. It is told that she ran back into the house, put a gun to her head and took her life.

Fast forward to the year 1977, to when The Expo Center was built on the same piece of land. At that time, I was conducting my tours out of the Executive Inn. The night watchmen and other people who worked at night were the best people to talk to about the place being haunted.

One night watchmen asked me one day, "Hey, have you ever heard about the Lady in White that haunts the Expo Center?"

"Nope," I replied.

He proceeded to tell me about when a *house of ill repute* stood on that same piece of land and about how poor Matilda had taken her life in that house. Of course, this actually was information that I already knew. The night watchmen continued to tell me a fascinating ghost story that happened to him and some

Pen It! Publications, LLC

David Wolfe

others.
This is his story:

> "One night my crew and I were up in the
> surveillance room watching the monitors, when
> something caught our eye. The Expo Center has
> a second floor which has international rooms on
> each side of its hallway. One part of the Expo
> Center has cameras pointing down this long
> creepy hallway. As we watchmen are watching
> the monitor we all of suddenly noticed
> something out of the norm."
>
> We saw a lady in a white wedding gown
> slowly walking down the hallway. We thought
> it was Matilda, still looking for her long lost
> love."

The men watching said that she was so
transparent that they could almost see through her.

There were no weddings that night, so it
couldn't have been an actual bride. As she walked
down the hallway, she suddenly disappeared.   The
men were stunned at what they had seen.

This Lady in White would turn up again in 2008,
when The Expo Center and the Big E were shut down
permanently. I knew a security guard named Josh,
who was all alone in the Big E after it was closed down.

Josh was walking the perimeter, making his
nightly rounds. He came to the area of the building
known as the *Showroom Lounge*. He claimed to hear a
woman's voice, however, nobody else was supposed to

be in the building. He slowly entered the room.

At one time, this room was hopping with music and variety acts. Many famous people performed on stage in this room: Waylon Jennings, The Oakridge Boys, Jerry Lee Lewis and more.

As Josh flashed his light all around, he shined it toward the stage. Suddenly, he saw a woman in white walking past the stage.

Josh said, "She looked as though she was trying to talk. As she walked by, I managed to pull out my cell phone and snap a picture of her. She suddenly disappeared, never to return."

Perhaps she was just saying good-bye to her former home or maybe she was looking for her long, lost love, one final time. The guard's photo made the front page news and caused a quite a stir around Owensboro. Many people didn't believe the picture was real. I was interviewed by the newspaper and asked my thoughts. I believed it.

Bob Green

The main building of The Big E had its own share of ghost stories. The Big E was built in 1977 by Bob Green. Mr. Green loved that building and he was quite proud of it. According to *Evansville Courier and Press,* Bob Green died in 1991 in a car accident in Indiana. After Mr. Green passed away, weird occurrences began happening around the establishment.

Pen It! Publications, LLC

One particular occurrence took place shortly after Mr. Green's death. A bartender who often served Mr. Green, when he was alive, told me that when Mr. Green would often buy people drinks in the *Time Out Lounge,* or at least show up to festive-up the place.

One night, as this bartender was working the bar, he happened to look up from wiping down a glass. To his astonishment, he saw Mr. Bob Green standing there! It looked as though he was either waving or toasting to the bartender. The bartender said he did a double take and Bob was gone.

This wasn't the only place where Bob hung out. Bob's old office used to be right around the front desk behind the staircase. Over time, that area was renovated into a ladies' restroom.

Some years after Bob's death, a lady manager had quite the experience. She went to use the facilities and was all alone inside of the restroom. She noticed through the cracks of the stall, that a man suddenly manifested out of nowhere! Obviously, this scared the young lady. She screamed and burst out of the stall, and the man disappeared. She reported the incident to security and they came to investigate, but found no one.

The security guards were aware of previous sightings of Bob and when they asked this lady manager to come with them and showed her a picture of Bob Green.

She yelled, "That's him! That's the man!"

The security guards didn't look too surprised. "Ma'am he's been dead for years now."

She said, "I don't care! That's who I saw!"

The security team told her that numerous other women had complained about that same occurrence. Apparently Bob was still taking care of business at his beloved Big E. Let's face it, it's his place and he can go wherever he pleases. Personally, I'm not saying that's who people have been seeing, but one thing I do know is that people have been seeing something or someone.

Big E Death Toll

It doesn't surprise me that the Big E is haunted. In doing my research, I noticed there had been multiple deaths inside of the Big E. I was once told there were fourteen deaths inside the Big E, from the time it was built in 1977 to its closing. Several of these were accidental deaths.

A man who was working on the 7th floor, fell to his death and landed on a table below, in the restaurant. This table happened to be where several lawyers normally sat to eat their meals. That's an odd coincidence, considering those particular lawyers represent only clients who have been involved in an accident. By the way, no lawyers were hurt during the fall, because no one was sitting there, at the time.

According to Judge Lanham, a horrible murder took place on the third floor. Two tool and die makers got into a fight at a convention they were attending, at the Big E. After the fight, one of the gentleman left and went to his room. Unbeknownst to him, the other gentleman had followed him, with a shotgun.

When someone knocked on the door, the first man peeked from behind the door, through the peephole and then he opened the door. The second man shot him, point blank.

Since that day, people who happen to be taking pictures of the area, would report numerous orbs present in their photos.

Other deaths were listed as natural deaths. For example, there were several elderly people who died in their rooms. Which brings me to my favorite story.

Room 2213 was reportedly one of the most haunted rooms in the building. An elderly woman and her husband were staying in this room. She was a diabetic. She had run out of insulin and had asked her husband to go down and get her some from the local pharmacy. When he came back, unfortunately, she had already passed on from a diabetic attack.

From that time on, the room was reportedly haunted. Those who stayed in room 2213 would claim that the sheets would be yanked vigorously from their beds. Other occupants would claim they heard a woman's voice faintly whispering, "Help....help..." Others would say they would hear footsteps walking back and forth, along with whispers for help.

One story relayed to me was very interesting. A front desk attendant said she was on the second floor when a gentleman in a very nice suit approached her and said, "Can you help me find the International Rooms?"

She responded that she would help him, and she escorted the man in the proper direction. As they were walking, the gentleman was right beside her, but said nothing more. As they continued down the hallway, her boss approached from the opposite end. He looked perplexed, as he approached her.

Once he reached her, he asked, "Where are you going?"

The attendant replied, "I'm taking this gentleman...."

She stopped mid- sentence and looked beside her. She swore he had been right beside her. He had disappeared into mid-air. She told me that if he had ducked behind a wall or gone into a room, she would have seen him do so.

In doing my research, I ran across a personal account of another ghost story on the website, *Topix*. This gentleman from the site said he worked as a person who picks up the trays.

This is his story, verbatim:

> "I used to work there as a room service employee from 03-05 and I tell ya at night, it was very creepy in some of those hallways. There was this one time in building 4, I was rushing because I was ready to go home. I had to pick up trays on one side of the hallway, because dayshift didn't do it that morning. I looked down the hallway, and the 4th building hallways always made me feel uneasy because

it looked like the Titanic hallways.

I was coming back from getting a tray, and this guy asked me why his key wouldn't work. I sat my tray on my cart and went to see if I could help him. I come back and no one was there. I wasn't gone but a few seconds, I thought maybe he got his key to work.

I rushed back to put my trays up so I could go home, and I had to take my bank money to the safe at the front desk. I asked them if someone could check out his room, he was having problems with his key. The woman laughed at me and said," No one is in that room."

I said, "OK, I'll get security down there then, to see if they can find him. I was clocking out and the older man security guard was on duty. I told him I thought someone was down there messing with rooms.

He said, "I saw you talking to yourself, down there."

I said, "Nah, I was helping someone."

He said, "Nah, you weren't. That's the ghost."

I was shocked, but this was not my only experience with the ghosts of the Big E, it was just my first experience."

As I conducted more research, I found that this tray collector had another story about the Big E ghost.

He continued, *"I got another one from the Presidential Suite on the 7th floor. I was picking up trays again, this time it was my own orders. It was about 10:30 at night, and I saw a housekeeper, this was when they had the Scandinavians housekeepers working. He asked me if I could help him for a second. Well, I had no problem helping a fellow co-worker. He was taking in bedsheets. We went into the suite and he was picking up trash and what-not. I checked the room service table inside the suite, just in case someone had not picked it up yet.*

If you've never been in that suite, it was kinda huge. I went towards the main bedroom and saw someone sitting in the rocker. I did a double take and they were gone. I asked the guy working with me if he had ever experienced anything similar.

He said, Yeah, but he calls them angels. I was like cool, picked up my tray and left."

I guess it's true that we entertain angels. I never knew that the guests and staff were being entertained by other ghostly guests.

I remember the Big E, as it's called, and seeing all the concerts and shows that came through. I used to love eating there and enjoyed the atmosphere. When you went there you felt like you were a part of the *Lifestyles of the Rich and Famous*. It was such a grand hotel and is missed very much.

The Owensboro Convention Center now stands

Pen It! Publications, LLC

where the Big E used to be. Who knows if the old haunts still linger around this new place.   Only time will tell.

Photo above taken from Josh the night Security guard on duty. It's supposedly the lady in white.

Chapter 3

Civil War Ghost/River Ghost

The American Civil War took place from 1861 to1865. Our town felt the impact just like numerous other towns throughout the nation. Owensboro was known to be a hotbed for confederate gorillas.

According to the Messenger-Inquirer 2002, in 1864 a Union Wharf boat pulled up to the banks of Owensboro. There were only 13 soldiers on this little wharf boat. Unknown to the Union Soldiers who set foot on the Owensboro River Banks, Confederates occupied the town. As Union soldiers were setting foot upon the banks, they were surrounded by Confederates. This band of Confederates were part of Captain Jack Bennett's guerillas. Union soldiers thought they'd be able to surrender, but instead they were executed. Their bodies were thrown on the wharf-boat and torches were cast upon it.

One gentleman who rode with Captain Bennett, Alfred Lafayette Dale, said that the Black Union Troop fired upon the Rebels as they were leaving. The Rebels turned to engage. The Union troops were part of the 108th Color Regiment. They were inexperienced in combat. Dale said they captured the wharf boat and killed all 13 of the union troops. The bodies were left on the boat, set a fire, and pushed down river. This

Pen It! Publications, LLC

was a ghastly scene, to say the least.

According to the newspaper, *The Monitor*, the men burned the boat, then killed a white officer and three black soldiers, who were defending the boat. Two were shot and thrown overboard. One charred set of remains was found onboard. The hull fire was put out. Those who put it out found three other black soldiers in the bottom of the boat, alive. They were begging to go back to their masters to work. They were afraid, and rightfully so.

Another boat story was found in the book *60 years of Owensboro.* It is said that in 1886 a boat called *The Mountain Boy* was leaving Cannelton, Indiana. When it got to approximately the same location where the Union wharf boat had its tragic end, *The Mountain Boy* hit a horrendous storm and capsized.

Many towns folk witnessed this happen and rushed to help the passengers get out of the water. Unfortunately, the captain's young son drowned, as well as, two deck hands.

Tragedy seems to follow the river front of Owensboro and so do ghost stories.

On one occasion, I interviewed a barge worker. Barge workers are often rolling down the river at what is known as, the ghost hour. The Ghost Hour is said to be between 2-6 am. Some call it the Witching Hour, or Hour of the Dead. During this time, the dead are supposedly more active. As this Barge worker was passing the Owensboro river edge, exactly where all this previous death had taken place, he noticed something strange in the water.

In our interview, he said, "I saw a Big Ball of Light in the water, as I looked over the edge of the boat. It was underneath the water and looked like it was trying to crest the water top. Each time it almost reached the water top, in would sink back down again. It did this about three times and then just blinked out."

I asked if he thought it was a buoy.

He said, "No way. Buoys float on top of the water, this was down in the water."

I asked him what he thought it was. The barge worker said he had heard tales of *The Mountain Boy* sinking and thought it was those poor souls trying to come up for one last breath of air. Or, he thought, maybe it was the ghost of the soldiers who were burned on the old Union wharf boat. Much like sailors have their ghost tales, barge workers carry their own tales.

I had also heard another tale from a customer of mine, a lady that worked at the Veterans of Foreign Wars (VFW). She saw a shining orb floating down the river at the same time of night, the ghost hour. She was taking a smoke break, and was looking east toward the river, just past the Blue Bridge. She noticed an orb-shaped light floating down the river. At first, she thought it was a barge. But, as it approached the area where the all the death occurred in the past, the light just went out!

She quickly went back inside, stunned by what she had witnessed.

During my research, I looked into river towns

that had been around for a long time, I noticed there has always been a lot of death......and ghosts!

The Courthouse

Photo of back of courthouse, taken by David Wolfe.

The Courthouse had its share of violence as a result of the Civil War, up close and personal. On January 2, 1865, our courthouse was burned down by a guerilla captain named, William Davidson. He had caught wind that a colored regiment had been stationed at our courthouse.

This didn't set well with him. He gathered 300 to 400 men together and charged Owensboro. Some say a brief skirmish ensued, but others say the Union troops retreated and left the town defenseless. Regardless of what happened, Captain Davidson rode up to the courthouse staff and told them that they had just a few minutes to get their records out of the courthouse and then he was going to burn it to the ground!

He was a man of his word and did just what he said he was going to do. According to the book, *Ladies of Civil War Owensboro.* they cast torches to the courthouse and the flames reached 80 feet high. When he was done, he left town.

I tell this story in order to share what happened to my tour group on a Halloween night. I had just finished telling this story and I had a ghost hunting item with me, called an Ovilus. This item allows any spirit that may wish to communicate to do so, through the use of the speaker on the device. Bear in mind that during this tour, we are in front of the courthouse. As I finished this story, the Ovilus turned on and audibly says, "Shot, hurt, pain, shot, hurt, pain!"

A member of the tour group caught an orb on camera while walking up the sidewalk toward the front door of the courthouse. All of our K2 meters, another ghost hunting item which lights up if it detects a ghost, turned on during this time.

The tour crowd exclaimed, "Mr. Wolfe, did you hear that!"

In a fearful voice, I replied, "Yes."

I still wonder if it was one of these soldiers who might have gotten shot in this alleged skirmish. *Who knows!* Maybe it was the ghost of Captain Davidson

Pen It! Publications, LLC

coming back to threaten us to didn't leave the area. I'll admit, I've got a big imagination, but with everyone in the group witnessing the events, there was no way I was imagining it.

Photo taken on Halloween night during the time the Ovilus went off. Could this be the ghost of a Civil War soldier?

Photo of the original courthouse before and after it burned.
From the Messenger Inquirer Sunday, July 19th, 1931 page 1 B.

Pen It! Publications, LLC

Chapter 4

The Courthouse Ghost and the Lynching Ghost

Hoodoo

We've already discussed our Civil War ghosts at the courthouse in our last chapter. But, this chapter has stories about the inside and back of the courthouse.

Unfortunately, Owensboro was notorious for lynching's. A couple of those lynching's actually happened on the courthouse lawn. This is not surprising because the old jail once stood directly behind the courthouse. This allowed them complete the tasks quickly and without having to travel very far.

The first story I want to talk about is Hoodoo. Most people associate Voodoo and Hoodoo with New Orleans. But, believe it or not, Owensboro had its own cases of Hoodoo.

According to *HOODOO, CONJURE, and ROOTWORK AFRICAN AMERICAN FOLK MAGIC* by Catherine Yronwode, "Hoodoo consists of a large body of African folkloric practices and beliefs with a considerable admixture of American Indian botanical knowledge and European folklore. Although most of its adherents are black, contrary to popular opinion, it has always been practiced by both whites and blacks in

America."

I find it most intriguing that we would have this here in Owensboro. But, it is considered a southern state and a river town.

The book *60 years of Owensboro* states that "in the year 1896, during Christmas week Owensboro had a Sheriff named Sheriff White. He was very well known and loved in Owensboro. One night, he was called out to a certain part of town to break up a fight. When he arrived at the scene, he was shot! His deputies arrived shortly thereafter and made an arrest."

One person they arrested was a gentleman named Alf Hoyt. According to the Book from which this story is derived (*60 years of Owensboro* by William Foster Hayes), Alf more than likely was not the culprit. He was known as a town drunk and not mentally competent. Keep in mind that in those days, tools used today to analyze crime scenes were not available.

Alf was jailed and had a couple hearings prior to his trial. His Lawyer was a Mr. Hayes. It was Christmas Eve when Mr. Hayes paid a visit to his client and delivered some bad news. Mr. Hayes informed Mr. Hoyt that he believed he was going to be hanged. That's a Christmas gift that I wouldn't want.

Mr. Hoyt said to Mr. Hayes as he was leaving, "I've thought of Somep'n we can maybe do."

Mr. Hayes replied, "What is it?"

Mr. Hoyt said, "Well, you know in another town there's a cullu'd man, that can Conjure."

"Can What?" Mr. Hayes asked.

"Can Conjure, he can Hoodo them" replied

Hoyt.

"I've already sent for him and I 'spect he will be here today."

I know the dialect is quite different than the way we speak today, so please bear with me.

Mr. Hayes tried to plead with him, but it fell on deaf ears. I guess Mr. Hoyt figured the conjurer could cast a spell on the judge and jury to change their minds. As Mr. Hayes left his client, he saw that he could not shake Mr. Hoyt 's faith in the Conjurer. As Mr. Hayes was leaving, he passed the jail waiting room, there sitting on a bench, was this Conjurer. Mr. Hayes asked him if that's who he was.

He simply replied, "Yes."

Mr. Hayes left him to talk again to Mr. Hoyt and asked him to do his Hoodoo magic.

As the clock struck midnight, a crowd converges on the old Jail. It's was a lynch mob! They broke into the jail and grabbed Alf Hoyt and hung him on a tree on the east side of the courthouse. Either the Hoodoo didn't have time to take affect or it was fruitless Hoodoo. Either way, it didn't work.

The Hanging of Dick May

Another hanging that took place in that same location, was in 1886. A gentleman by the name of Dick May was hanged. He was accused of a crime, but never convicted. His jailer, Mr. Lucas, went to his death trying to ward off the lynch mob. An Old West type of shootout ensued and poor Mr. Lucas was shot trying to keep the lynch mob from taking Mr. May. In the end, the efforts of Mr. Lucas did not endure. Mr. May was hanged.

The Lynching Tree

Let me tell you about a tree, which is located on the back side of the courthouse. Some say it's the lynching tree. Others say the old tree was on the east side and is no longer standing. What is odd, is many times people on my Ghost Tour would take pictures of the tree and strange orbs would appear. The orbs were always hanging from the limbs of the tree.

Guests of my ghost tours have also witnessed Ectoplasm mist, and it is always around that tree. Ectoplasm is like the ghost itself, trying to manifest. Again, this mist was always hanging from the limbs. Some say it is the ghost of Dick May or Alf Hoyt still hanging around, trying to prove their innocence. Or maybe they just want justice. I will say we have had odd occurrences around that tree.

Even if it's not paranormal, strange things tend to go on there. Most of the time on my tour, I'll hand out my EMF Detectors. They always start lighting up when I talk about the lynching. It is as if the spirits are trying to tell us their version of the story.

One time on the tour, I had a very large group. We were behind the courthouse and as I finished telling a story, my group and I noticed the head of a figure peak around some pillars near the door. The crowd asked me if I had seen the figure. I replied that I had and I ran up there right after seeing it. I went up to investigate, there was no one there. The doors were locked. We were convinced we would have seen the doors open, but they did not. Very strange indeed!

Photo taken by David Wolfe.

Top two Photos taken by a tourist on my ghost tour. Note: the orbs hanging from the tree and the above Photo has green mist.

The Sheriff's Office

The inside of the courthouse also has its share of stories. The book *60 years of Owensboro* claims that, Around the turn of the century, a Deputy Jones and a Sheriff Wilson were all alone one night, sleeping on the second floor. They were awakened by a strange sound. It was the sound of footsteps coming down the hallway. These footsteps kept getting louder and louder and louder! Finally, they were at the doorway of the Sheriff's office. Then a loud thud was heard. It sounds like someone's body had dropped to the floor.

The two men had their hands on their guns. They thought someone had broken in and was coming

Pen It! Publications, LLC

after them. They turned on the light and rushed out the doors to find their intruder. They threw open the door and found nothing. Immediately, the sounds ceased.

While researching this information, I uncovered information that what they actually did find was that a few weeks prior to their experience, a drifter named Mr. Angel had been walking down the hallway. He was a healthy middle-aged man. He was trying to make his way to the Sheriff's office. As he finally approached the doorway, he collapsed and suddenly died. There was no apparent reason for his death!

No one knows why, to this day, what killed Mr. Angel. Yet today, people still hear the ghost of Mr. Angel trying to get to the old Sheriff's office. The loud footsteps can be heard walking, ever-so-slowly, to the office. Until it finally stops with a loud thump!

Mabel Is Here

Another popular ghost story is about a lady named Mabel. The story was told to me by a lady named Mrs. P. She proceeded to tell me that doors throughout different offices would open and shut on their own. Most of the office workers knew the story and would just ignore it and say, "Oh Mabel's here."

A lady that joined us on my tour back in 2010 and called me to say she thought she had physically seen our Mabel.

I said, "Please do tell."

She said, "One day I had gone into the courthouse and went into the ladies' restroom. I was the only one in there and when I went to wash her hands, I noticed that there was. no one in the stalls. I could have seen the door, if anyone had been coming in. I bent down to wash my hands and gradually rose my eyes up to look into the mirror. All of the sudden a lady with demonic eyes was staring back at me instead of my own reflection. I whipped around to look behind me. No one was there, and so I looked back into the mirror. The lady with demonic eyes was gone! I ran out of the restroom, scared and confused."

One story passed down to me by a customer, said that a worker died in the basement while working on the newer building, in the 1960's. Supposedly, this worker was standing near his scaffolding, when he rose up and hit it with his head. This scaffolding had a heavy tool laying on it. It fell off and hit him in the head, killing him instantly.

A ghost hunting group filmed in the basement one time and captured a green mist floating in the exact spot where this worker had died. Whenever I am in the basement, my EMF detectors go off in that same spot, but they do not go off anywhere else. If nothing else, it is a very odd coincidence.

So, if you go into the courthouse, be sure to say hello to Mabel. Let Mr. Angel just pass you by if you hear the phantom footsteps heading towards the sheriff's office. Based on these haunting experiences, I would say that both the inside and outside of the courthouse are very haunted areas.

Pen It! Publications, LLC

Chapter 5

Haunted Houses

Montgomery House

Photo taken by Chris Smith.

There's a house on St. Elizabeth Street called the Montgomery House and it is rich with history. Built in 1875, one legend is that the house was once a brothel. It's labeled so, because the street directly behind it is Mulberry Street. Mulberry Street was famously known to be the center of the Red Light District.

In all of my research, the only evidence I found close to attest to this, is that in the 1890's a Mrs.

Edwards owned the house and ran it as a boarding house. Maybe she rented rooms out to working ladies. We will never know.

The biggest piece of history I have found regarding the house, is in 1932. Mrs. Montgomery acquired the house and lived there until 1977. She lived in the house longer than any other occupant, thus giving it the name it has today: The Montgomery House

Mrs. Montgomery once owned the famous Velvet Ice Cream Company and had the reputation of being a hard working lady. She was known to stay at work late in the evening, until the last truck came in.

Years after she owned the house, the building was renovated into apartments and later the Tourist Commission office.

In 2006, it was Gordons Law Office. I began my research by going into this law office to ask questions about the property. When you approach these supposedly haunted places, you cannot simply barge into the buildings and ask, "Got ghosts?" like the "Got Milk?" commercials. They will absolutely show you the front door.

I approached cautiously and asked the group of lawyers about the history of the building. Then ever-so delicately, I asked if anything odd had ever happened in the house. Everyone said, in unison, "No, Mr. Wolfe, nothing here." Just as I was about to leave, a young intern raised her hand and said, "Mr. Wolfe I had something happened to me one night."

I must have rubbed my hands together like a

mad scientist, as I asked her, "Do tell."

She told me that one night she was asked to come in to work on some reports that were due. She entered the big, beautiful, but creepy home, all alone. She walked to her desk, which is located in the front, and sat down to work. She said she was looking around and noticed that on this particular night, it was dead calm; no pun intended.

Most old houses creak and pop because of settling, but not this night. Surprisingly, out of nowhere, the house begins to shake and then there are three loud BOOM, BOOM, BOOM, sounds! The young lady got up from her chair and thought to herself, "What in the world was that?"

On a side note, I'm not sure I would have waited for that third BOOM!

Like something from a bad horror movie, she heads toward the sound. In most horror movies they hide in the attic, shower, or basement. This is just asking for trouble.

This young lady continues down into the basement. She put her hand on the doorknob and slowly turned it to the left. As though the house was responding to her again, she heard Boom! Boom! Boom! This time she ran out of the house and refused to work there alone, ever again. To this day, no one knows what made that earth-shattering sound.

During a tour, one Halloween night when I told this story, there was a little old lady in the crowd. She yelled, "Mr. Wolfe!" and pointed her long, thin finger toward the top window, in front of the house. She said in a creepy voice, "I can tell you that place is haunted."

I asked, "How's that?" Not knowing the response I'd get.

She said, "I used to live there when it was apartments."

The whole crowd's jaws dropped. No one said a word. I was like a kid in a candy store. I said, "Oh, please tell us your story."

She said she lived downstairs when it was divided into apartments. She told us no one lived in the apartment above her and for good reason. She said, "Many nights I would hear this scraping and clawing sound. It sounded like someone was dragging a dead body."

Later, I happened to interview another lady who worked at the same building, when it was the Tourist Commission. When I asked her about the sounds described by this little old lady, she went pale and said," Mr. Wolfe, she's not lying. I too would hear that scraping and clawing sound in the same room."

It turns out that she had keys to the room, but when she went to investigate, she found nothing. In fact, the sound stopped when she entered. From their recollection, there were no pets, mice, and no rat infestation in this building. Whatever it was, is still a mystery.

On that same night that the little old lady told us her tale about the apartment above her, there was a ghost hunting group called P.A.S.T. that was on the same tour. It so happened, that they had a temperature gauge with them, with a red laser light. Coincidentally, they were pointing it the same room we were talking about.

The theory is that if spirits are around, the temperature tends to drop or fluctuate. They motioned me to come over to them.

They said, "Watch this." They pointed outside and the temperature was about 50 degrees. They pointed up at the room on the second floor and it dropped in temperature about 20 degrees. What's strange about this, is there is no power into the place. There could be no window air conditioner unit in a window to that room or anything else causing the fluctuation in temperature.

Some say. it always feels like someone is standing there looking out the window, staring down at us. My wife, who's been on the tour numerous times, says she hates that house. She feels the same way, like someone's staring at us out that window. If it was a brothel, who knows what atrocities happened in there that may cause these disturbances.

Photo of the Montgomery house with an Orb. The Haunted room is the two windows on the second floor. Taken by David Wolfe.

Pen It! Publications, LLC

Haunted Row:

The pic above is the Gilliam/Hopkins house taken by David Wolfe.

The Gilliam Hopkins House

On West 7th Street is a road I call, Haunted Row. I call it this because there are three houses in row on this street that are all rumored to be haunted. The first one is called, The Gilliam Hopkins House. I always thought it looked like the house from the Halloween Movies, you know, the Michael Myers House. It's that creepy.

Courthouse Records state that it was built by

Dr. Gilliam in 1890. He lived in the home for only a few years. He then passed it on to his son.

The interesting history about this house is that when Rainey Bethea committed the murder he was hanged for; this house was where he lived.

Records in the Kentucky Room state the lady who lived there in 1936 boarded out rooms. Rainey was one of her tenants. In 1959, The Hopkins family acquired the house. This leads to our ghost stories.

I knew the Hopkins family. I used to work with their son, Tim. I went to visit them one night at this creepy, old home. As we were watching wrestling on TV, Tim asked me if I would like to hear a ghost story. Now, I didn't think he was going to talk about the house I was in, so as I'm looking over my shoulder and counting my goosebumps, I listened.

Tim said that in the 1980's, he and his friend had a couple girls who they were supposed to pick up for a date. Tim's friend was in the house with him. Tim told him to wait downstairs while he went upstairs to take a shower, then they could leave. As Tim's friend was sitting watching TV, he said he suddenly got this funny feeling he was being watched. He very slowly looked over his right shoulder, when he saw something out of the normal. The men were alone in the house. But, he saw this lady in white, slowly walk down the stairs. Then she started to walk toward Tim's friend. She looked like her arms were reaching out for him. Tim said his friend jumped to his feet and slammed out the front door, screaming. When Tim got out of the shower and came downstairs, he noticed his friend was gone.

Tim called him on the telephone and said, "Where are you? We've got to go!"

His friend said," I'm never stepping foot into that house again."

Tim laughed and his friend said, "What's so funny?"

Tim said, "Oh you've seen her too."

"Too?" his friend asked.

Tim said, "She has been spotted numerous time in the past. My dad has even seen her when he shaves in the morning."

Tim's dad said he would be shaving and look behind him in the mirror. He would then see a lady in white standing there and then suddenly she would vanish.

Tim's brother, Stephen, once had quite a fright during the daytime. He was on the phone with his fiancée, who is now his wife. He said he heard an awful noise in one of the rooms upstairs. He told his fiancée to get ready to call the cops. He thought someone had broken in upstairs. Stephen ran upstairs to the room where the sound had come from.

This room had two doors. He went to the front door of the room, and it felt like someone was holding the door back, trying to keep him from entering. He went to the other door. He knew that this door had a bookshelf in front of it on the other side. He pushed the door with all his might and managed to break past that door. Once inside, what he saw astonished him.

All the furniture was stacked in the middle of

the room in a circle-type pattern. He said it was very weird. It must be noted there was no storms, earthquake, or no tornadoes in the area that day. All of the windows were shut. Whatever it was, must of not liked the furniture where it was at.

Mr. Dixon who is the current owner of the house also had a fright. He said he was working late in a room of the house, which is located on the second floor. He came down the stairs; the same stairs that had the lady in white on it, and as he made the last step, he looked into the living room and saw a glowing, greenish orb. It was just hovering there in midair. It was as though the orb had seen him, and suddenly, it shot into the other room.

Mr. Dixon said out loud, "I'm not here to hurt you. I'm here to fix your house." Then Mr. Dixon walked quickly out of the house.

My group LIG, Adam Forsyth, Brad McNeal, and myself were privileged to get to investigate this house. The evidence we caught was most intriguing. On the EVPs, which stands for Electronic Voice Phenomenon it is a recording on a dicta-phone, we caught a voice on the stairs saying, "Get out!" At the same time, one of our member's backpack was pulled, as he stood on the staircase. We also caught what sounded like a baby crying. That recording gave me the creeps.

What's really weird about that, was Stephen Hopkins said he was awakened one night to the sound of labored breathing. At the time, Stephen stepped out into the hallway and found nothing, and just as suddenly as it had begun, the breathing stopped. I often wonder if the sound of a baby screaming and labor breathing were connected. I found no research to prove or disapprove this awful sound.

Other Homes on Haunted Row

Mr. Dixon's house is another house on Haunted Row. He says that he has a ghost that tends to wander around. It will open the basement door and then travel upstairs. It will then open one of the bedroom doors. Mr. Dixon is used to the strange occurrences and says he thinks nothing of them.

The third house, the house next door to Mr. Dixon, has a few more strange events. It was built and once owned by a Dr. Brown, back in the 1890s. It is beautiful looking home that reminds you of a dollhouse.

The previous owners told me they experienced a weird phenomenon one night. The young couple were going out on a date one winter night. They closed the doors upstairs to conserve heat. When they came home, what they saw shocked them. All the drawers in the kitchen were opened. All the cabinets were opened and the door upstairs were back open again. The couple were stunned, but just shut all the opened drawers and doors. They never talked about it again until I asked them whether they had any experiences.

Mr. Dixon told me that before that couple owned the house, another occurrence took place. A gentleman was doing some remodeling in the home and was there alone. He was a big, strong guy who didn't look like he spooked easily. He was working on the first floor, when he heard something or someone, walking from room to room. It was quite loud. Then next, it sounded like they were running.

The man who was remodeling ran outside and straight next door to Mr. Dixon's house. He banged on the door, vigorously.

Mr. Dixon came to the door and asked, "How can I help you?"

The gentleman told him in a frightened voice what he had heard. They went back to the house together to investigate. They found nothing at all: no noise and nobody walking around. The gentleman thanked Mr. Dixon and left, never to return. With tales like these, you can see why I call it Haunted Row.

Above is Dr. Brown's home on Haunted Row. Photo taken by David Wolfe

Haley McGinnis Funeral Home

Stirmans folly/Haley McGinnis funeral home photo taken by David Wolfe

The Haley McGinnis Funeral Home was built by Dr. Stirman in 1860. It is loosely called Stirman's Folly. The reason for this is, it was originally supposed to be four stories tall. When the American Civil War broke out, he only got three stories built.

A Mr. Ewing took over the home in 1915 and had a very important historical figure visit the home one night. Mrs. Clara Barton came to the home one night, for a ball. She is the founder of the Red Cross and a was a nurse during the Civil War.

According to the website, http://www.haleymcginnis.com/who-we-are/history-and-staff, it wasn't until 1966 that Haley McGinnis consolidated its services to include the Owensboro Funeral Home. This merger made Haley McGinnis Funeral Home and Crematory the premier home to call on during a family's time of need.

I love this beautiful home and, in fact, that's where I want my funeral to take place, when that time comes.

There are tales about this place being haunted, nothing malicious, though. There are stories of phantom footsteps being heard in the upstairs. I once heard a story of an apparition of an old couple who appeared upstairs. I'm not sure if those stories are true or not, but the stories I'm going to tell now, are indeed true.

These stories come from a lady named, Shirlene, who worked next door. She had some really interesting things happen to her when she moved in the place.

Shirlene moved into the building right above the funeral home. The first night she moved into the place, she was awakened at 2:00 a.m. to the sound of chairs being moved about in the lounge. This happened for several nights in a row. Each time, there was no one there.

After about the third night, she went to the staff, who worked there, and asked, "Okay, who has been down in the lounge below me moving chairs at 2:00 a.m.?"

The staff jus grinned and someone said, "Oh, you didn't know this, but the place is haunted."

Another experience took place when Shirlene's

son came home one night, after working late at a bar. He went out to the terrace to take a break and unwind. As soon as he entered the terrace, the door locked behind him. This wasn't one of those doors that would accidentally lock by itself. You literally had to turn the lock to lock it. He had the lock turn by itself. He had to call his mom on her cell phone to come down and unlock the door. This was the first time, but it happened to him on numerous occasions.

Another happening occurred when Shirlene was in her office in the building, on the left of the funeral home. She said she was working in her office, when she saw a big, black cat walking from room to room. She thought it was odd, since all the doors were shut. She got up to look for the cat, but it had vanished. She went upstairs to the apartment and asked them if they had a black cat. They looked at her and smiled.

Shirlene asked, "Oh, no. What now?"

They said, "You probably didn't know this, but this house is haunted by a black cat."

Shirlene thought to herself, "Now they tell me."

The best story of them all, happened to the attendants who lived in the main building. They had the whole second floor to themselves. One night, about 2:00 a.m., a loud knock sounded on their door.

The lady heard, "Owensboro Police Department. Open up!"

She did as she was asked. She asked the officer, "Can I help you?"

The office responded, "Yes ma'am, we got a

911 call from the main building. We need to investigate.

She tried to call the gentleman who lived there, but no one answered the call. The officers were very persistent that they needed into the building. They entered with guns drawn. They went upstairs and knocked on the door. The officers woke up the other tenants and told them the same story about the 911 call.

One gentleman responded, "You woke us up for that, no one called you.

They looked throughout the home and found nothing malicious. The next night the same thing happened, at the exact same time. This took place so many times, that finally the Owensboro Police Department had a detective look into the matter. What he found was most startling.

After the investigation, the police came to Shirlene's door and told her what they found.

The officer said, "The OPD did a trace on the number and found out that it is an old phone number and is no longer in service. It belonged to a lady who used to live in the building back in the 1970's. She died there at the old home.

She did not have to go far for her funeral. Apparently, she was calling from beyond the grave.

The Campbell Club

The Campbell Club, Photo taken by David Wolfe.

Pen It! Publications, LLC

Photo taken by David Wolfe.

The next home I'm telling you about, is one of the most unique looking homes I have ever seen. The history record at the Campbell Club states, *It's part of the Second Empire architectural styles.* It was built in 1880 by John Woolfolk. It is documented that a distant cousin to President Andrew Jackson, once owned the house. His name was C. D. Jackson. After Mr. Jackson, Dr. Gilliam owned it until it became a retirement home. This makes me wonder who may have died in the home.

In 1959, Harry Holder of Holder Ford Company, turned it into, the *Campbell Club*. It is a private eating club, for members only. However, I believe they now open their doors to the public.

Mr. Matt Weafer is the manager and head chef of the place, and a good friend. I've done a couple historical shows at this beautiful place and the food is excellent and the service is great! I invite you to go into the establishment and say hello to the staff and their resident ghost.

The first ghost story I heard about this place, was a great one to start with There was a waitress who was walking by a particular room they have always called the *President's Room*. In this room there was a little radio. At this particular time, the radio was turned off.

Just as the lady approached the doorway, the radio turned on and blasts out loud! She didn't think anything about it, at the time, so she turned off the radio and went about her business.

She made her way past the *President's Room* again and just as she arrived at the doorway, suddenly, the radio turned on again. Once again it blasts out loud.

She was a little spooked, to say the least, but thought maybe it was just a power surge. However, as she passed by the *President's Room* again later, the radio turned on once again, blaring music out, even louder!

This time, as she went back into the room, to turn the radio off, she noticed something very odd. When she bent over to flick the off switch, she noticed the radio was unplugged.

She said out loud, "Whoever you are, I am never going past this door again, nor will I go into this room." And, she did not, for the rest of the night.

There is no research to prove who this

Pen It! Publications, LLC

phantom person was, but apparently, this particular ghost likes to listen to music.

Another time, a co-worker was going up stairs to the third floor, one evening, to retrieve an item. Matt saw him come down the stairs and he was white as a ghost. When asked what was wrong, the coworker explained what had happened.

He said, "I went upstairs to retrieve something, and when I started to come back down the stairs, the door on the third floor slammed all by itself. I tried to reopen the door, but it was as if someone was holding the door back. I then ran downstairs, quickly!"

Other workers said they had same thing happened to them. Some even say the door opens by itself, too. Everyone who works there now has a hard time going up to the third floor.

Another story takes place in one of the dining rooms, where a lone waitress, Jackie, was locking up and getting ready to leave. Jackie had pushed in all the chairs under the tables and left the room. As Jackie was getting ready to leave, she walked past the dining room on her way out and she noticed something out of the normal. All of the chairs were pulled back out! No one came in behind her and no one was left in the dining room. Jackie pushed in the chairs again and left. Apparently the phantom customers weren't done eating.

Chelsea, another worker, said that when you come into this place and you don't say, "Hello, Mary," odd things will happen to you.

Matt has had a few odd things that have

happened, right from the start of his employment. The first morning he went in to work, Matt went to the bar to get something to drink. This was around the 5 a.m. Matt knew we was all alone in the home but, all of the sudden, he heard a person whistling throughout the house. He was spooked and Matt exited immediately. He waited for another staff member to show up before going back in.

Another time, Matt was working and he had placed some food in a blender. He said that out of nowhere, the blender picked up in midair and dumped over. I guess the ghost didn't like what Matt was preparing.

The last story Matt told me, was about one night when he was coming down the grand staircase. It was closing time and every customer had left. As he came down the stairs and passed one of the dining rooms, he saw a lady sitting by the window looking out. He went to the back of the restaurant and asked the staff who the lady customer was in the front dining room.

They replied," No one is here. Everyone's gone."

When they all went back to the front dining room to have a look, the lady had vanished.

A lot of women complain in the room about feeling, as though they are being watched. That same dining room is adjacent to the lady's restroom. The legend is a lady hung herself in that room.

Matt and the staff have said that when they close up at night and are all alone, they would hear people walking down the stairs.

Matt's wife said that she was in the house one night and she heard someone screaming. It sounded as though it was coming from upstairs.

Matt has told me a disturbing tale about his son. The young boy was playing upstairs, by himself, on the second floor. He was only three-years-old, when this took place. He came to his dad and said he liked playing with the little boy in the back room. Matt was surprised since there was no one there.

A couple of years later, when Matt's son was five years old, he suddenly wasn't too happy to go up there in the room. Matt said he heard his son crying. He went to find him.

When he finally located the boy, Matt asked, "What's wrong."

He responded," The little boy is angry at me and doesn't want to play with me anymore. His son didn't go into the room again.

There were a couple different ghost hunts conducted inside the club. One ghost hunter caught, a voice on an EVP. It was captured near the bar and the voice said," I'll take another drink." What an appropriate place for that statement.

Another ghost hunter claimed to catch a man in a mirror, who was looking back him. Yet another ghost hunter claimed he saw a big, black mass form, right in front of him. It was in a room off from the bar. When his co-hunter met up with him, he looked like he seen a ghost. When he conveyed his experience, they both left the room rather quickly.

There seem to be a lot of hauntings in this beautiful, majestic home.

The Miller House

Photo above taken by David Wolfe of the Miller house

There is a big, beautiful home located on 5th and J. R. Miller Streets that was built by Elmer Miller in 1905. According to the *Miller House website* and *The Messenger Inquirer,* the following text is a short history of the building.

As written in the Messenger Inquirer in the summer of 1905: described the plans for the elaborate home of Elmer and Lizzy Miller, located at Fifth and Lewis, which is now J. R. Miller Blvd.

In 1905, Elmer Miller obtained a mold by Sears, Roebuck, and Company to make 1,800 artificial stone blocks for his home. He hauled sand for the blocks up the Ohio River during construction. Referred to as, *the prettiest and most conveniently arranged home in the city*, this home cost around $8000. This was a substantial amount, for its day. Beside the home, stood a carriage house erected for Elmer's electric automobile, said to be the first of its type in town.

Elmer was a prominent business man. He founded the *Miller Coal and Contracting Company*, in the late 1880s. The company expanded to transfer and hauling, and then they began building roads. Elmer Miller laid several miles of road in Daviess County. He served on the City Council and was a member of the Rotary Club and the Chamber of Commerce.

Lizzy Miller was a member of the Women's Club and a leader in Red Cross activities during WWI. Both Elmer and Lizzy Miller were very charitable. As active members of First Christian Church, the couple donated leftover stones to the church, during construction, in 1905. Elmer sent many loads of coal to those in distress and otherwise helped those in need. In additional to their many contributions to Owensboro, Elmer and Lizzy Miller built a home which would later be called 'A Jewel of Old Owensboro'.

Elmer Miller passed away in 1922 at the age of fifty-six. Lizzy Miller lived in their home for twenty more years. Neighbors describe her as a generous woman who made chicken soup and molasses pie for those who were sick in the neighborhood.

In the late 1960s and 1970s the home was turned into several apartments and housed various owners and tenants. However, the home was on the brink of a rebirth.

" Larry and Jeanie Kirk bought the old home and remodeled it. They saved this beautiful home from ultimate deterioration. The Kirks turned it into one of the finest restaurants in the tri- state area. What they didn't know was when they bought the home, it came with previous occupants.

There are reports of three deaths surrounding the house. The first one was Clyde, the gardener. Poor Clyde was going home one day after a long day of working. I would assume, from working the yard around the home. I was told by the owner, that Clyde was found the next day in the alley behind the house. He was murdered and no one knows who murdered Clyde.

The next death took place when the house was used as a boarding home for local women who worked at Ken-Rad factory, which was just down the road. A gentleman came calling one night, to visit one of the girls who lived there.

The lady manager of the house, came home and startled the young couple. The gentleman caller leapt out the top window, thinking he could make the jump. Unfortunately, he was mistaken and he leapt to his death. He died as a result of injuries he received in the landing.

The last death of record, occurred during the time when the home was very run down and had been abandoned. A gentleman, who was either homeless or on drugs, was found dead in the home, by the police.

Pen It! Publications, LLC

One can see that a few tragedies happened inside and around the home. One could see why it's said to be haunted.

Jeanie Kirk told me the stories that follow. One day their daughter was sitting on the front porch of the Miller House. She said that out of nowhere she saw a woman at the front door peak out and then duck back inside. Their daughter, Megan, said her hair was a dark color. She was an older woman and was dressed in old fashioned clothing. She had a long dress, with her hair pulled back in a bun.

Could this be the ghost of Mrs. Miller, checking to see who was on her porch?

One lady who was working on the beautiful stain glass window, located on the top of the home, came to visit one day. She went up to the house and noticed it was locked. She knocked on the front door, hoping someone would be home.

She hollered, "Hello." She wasn't expecting a response. Clearly the house empty or so she thought.

A lady's voice yelled back," I'll be right there!" This startled the young glass maker and she left.

She later relayed the story to Jeanie Kirk. Mrs. Kirk claimed that this phantom lady ghost even called her name out loud at times.

Aaron King was a bartender at the Miller House and he too had strange ghostly encounters. I interviewed Aaron King and these are the stories he relayed to me.

Aaron said the first experience he had was one night when he was bartending. He was standing behind the bar, talking to the people who were sitting at the bar.

He said," We have wine glass racks that hang overhead, behind the bar. As we were talking, one of the wine glasses fell from the middle of the rack. If you look at the design of the rack you can tell it's not possible for the glass to enter, or exit the rack unless it is from the end. I looked at the glass after it fell, and after falling that far, the only thing that had broken was the stem of the glass."

He told me in the interview that they all got kind of freaked out after that.

Another experience that happened to Aaron, involved being behind the bar and a glass.

Aaron said," The Miller House has several small glasses, which are used for bourbon. They are called Glencairin Glasses." He continued, "I had been washing them behind the bar, and then putting them upside down on a mat on top of the bar. I was talking to a customer, when in my peripheral vision, I saw a glass flip from upside down to right side up! I immediately looked at Larry Kirk, the Owner, who was sitting at the end of the bar and asked him, "Did you see that?"

Larry replied," I did," and continued drinking.

The last experience that happened to Aaron, was probably the one that freaked him out the most. Aaron said he came to the Miller House late one night, around 10:30 p.m. to 11 p.m., to do bar inventory.

Aaron said, "At night you hear all kinds of things like creeks and pops." He had become accustomed to the sounds the old house made. This particular night, he was in the basement, where the bar is located. He was counting beer bottles, when out of nowhere he heard the front door open and then shut, and then heard footsteps walking across the floor.

Aaron went upstairs to see who had come in. No one was there, and the front door was still locked. So, Aaron went back downstairs to continue his count. This time, he heard footsteps and then he heard them stop at the top of the basement stairs. He walked to the bottom of the basement stairs and looked up.

Suddenly he heard a woman's voice say to him, "Baby!"

"This scared me," Aaron claimed. Before panicking, he called his girlfriend, Abby. Abby worked at the club and was also the daughter of Larry and Jeanie Kirk, who had keys to the place. He thought maybe she had dropped by. She answered the phone when he called and claimed she was never there.

"This scared me to death!" Aaron said. After that, he turned on the radio and blasted music loudly, to drown out any phantom footsteps.

. I was alone at the place, except for Aaron, and was investigating the building. Aaron was in the bar, down in the basement. I investigated for a while, but didn't get much of anything, so I went downstairs to tell Aaron I was leaving.

Out no nowhere, we both heard the chairs on the second floor move, as if someone was rearranging furniture above us.

I looked at him and said, "Did you hear that?"

He just smiled like it was normal. I ran back upstairs and found nothing abnormal. All the chairs were pushed in properly. I went back downstairs and was telling Aaron that all was well, when we heard it again.

This time, I looked at him and said, 'Well, I'm done for the night."

He smiled, told me to have a good night, and turned his music back up.

Pen It! Publications, LLC

Chapter 6

Bill's

Photo taken by David Wolfe.

The building, now known as *Bill's*, was built in 1920 and was previously known as, the *Calluis Sweet Shop*, which primarily sold candy. The building sits next to the old Malco Theatre, now home to The Theatre Workshop. Beginning in the 1960's through 2010, it was home to *Barney's Restaurant*. They had great food and always packed a crowd.

When Bill acquired the building he turned it into a classy, elegant diner offering great food and great service.

Our story concerning haunts of Bill's, take place with the previous owner, Naomi. Naomi told me the mystery of the *ghost dime*. There is a dime that mysteriously and continuously shows up at this certain table in the back of the diner.

Naomi said her daughter, Wendy, would help clean the place at closing time. Wendy was very meticulous and always made sure the place was super clean. Wendy would have noticed if anything had been left on the floor. She worked diligently cleaning and went home this particular evening.

The next day, when Wendy or a waitress would come in to open the place they would find a dime on the floor. It was always back by the same table, every morning. They would pick the dime up each morning and place it in the cash register. Sure enough, the next day, it would return. Bill claims the same thing happened to him and his workers, once he acquired the building. In fact, they gave me one of the ghost

Pen It! Publications, LLC

dimes, which I have still, and it still shows up at the diner.

Another story at Bill's, involves objects moving on their own. Glasses or other items have disappeared and then suddenly, reappeared at another location in this establishment.

Naomi revealed her best ghost story to me. It took place one night, when she was in the basement, all alone. She was counting the day's money and doing some office work.

Naomi said, "Out of nowhere, I hear every dish in the kitchen, come crashing down on the first floor."

The doors were locked, but she thought someone had broken in. She raced upstairs.

I asked her, "Did you find your dishes everywhere?"

Naomi said, "That's the weird thing. All of the dishes were completely safe and still up on the shelves."

The next night, Naomi was in the basement again, doing the same thing. When she heard her dish cart being pushed and pulled down the middle aisle on the first floor. She went upstairs again, thinking she would finally find something or someone.

I asked," Did you find your dish cart?"

Naomi said," No, it was perfectly locked away in the closet."

The third night was the charm. Naomi's daughter, Wendy, was in the basement counting the day's money, this time. Suddenly, Wendy got this feeling of being watched. She said that a cold chill ran over her and the hair on her neck stood on end. She heard an angry voice behind her!

"WENDY! WENDY! WENDY!"

Wendy ran out of the diner, screaming and left the money and all sitting on the desk. She told Naomi that she was never closing alone again.

When Bill opened the diner, he too had strange experiences. Of course, they had the ghost dime constantly reappearing, but things got even stranger.

One eerie event involved a donation jar which sat on the bar. The staff would leave the room for some reason, and upon returning, they find the jar on the other side of the bar. Now, that's a long journey for this jar to take! I tried to debunk this, thinking maybe it was possibly caused by condensation. Water will make glasses move on their own once, they get the surface wet from condensation. But, after careful examination, I found that the bard was dry, and the jar would have to move straight, then turn, go straight and turn again, to reach its destination. It made no sense why this jar would move. Eventually, they put a brick on the jar, and it finally stopped moving.

Another occurrence happens when various materials, not all the same type, vanish and reappear in other areas of the diner. This is much the same as the occurrences at several other places I have investigated. This too, is a common phenomenon.

One particular morning, Bill's fiancée' came in alone, to open up. She thought she saw someone peek around the corner of the basement, as she went by. She paid no mind, thinking she was seeing things. She proceeded upstairs and upon entering the office, she saw the blinds moving up completely on their own. It was as though some disembodied hands were pulling them. She left quite quickly.

My favorite story that the staff at Bill's told me, took place one morning when a couple of the cooks came into the diner. They were completely alone. As they entered dining room, they heard someone walking upstairs above them. They thought maybe their friend had gotten there early and was up there walking around. So, they went outside to take a smoke break. To their surprise, guess who showed up? Their friend!

They said, "We thought you were already here."

They all three went together upstairs to investigate, and found no one. This uneasy feeling stuck with them all day.

Bill showed me a very odd looking scratch on a wall, that he said appeared out of nowhere. It appeared to be three claw marks. The marks are located above the wall when you are going down the basement stairs.

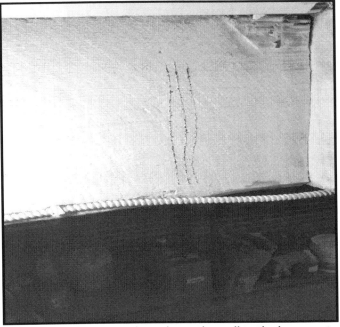

Photo of the three scratch marks on the wall to the basement at Bill's restaurant. Photo taken by David Wolfe.

The picture above shows these scratches, and I must say, they look very intimidating. Bill said one day they weren't there and then suddenly, they were.

I noted that the scratches are too far up for an animal to claw up there and there seemed to be no reason for them to have appeared. If there had been an animal that made the scratches, there should be a series of claw marks, not just one set. I was just as perplexed as Bill was over the origin of these marks.

Back when the building was *Barney's*, I personally had an experience that left me perplexed. I went into Barny's to pick up a takeout order. As you

Pen It! Publications, LLC

entered the diner, and, look up, you will notice a series of overhead chandeliers. I was standing at the bar waiting for my food, when I noticed something out of place. One of the chandeliers was rocking very hard, by itself, while all the other ones were perfectly still. I decided to try to debunk this.

I went upstairs thinking that perhaps someone was stomping up and down on that particular spot. No one was up there. So then, I thought, maybe it had been an earthquake. But, if that were the case, all the other chandeliers would also be moving. I couldn't figure it out, and it was still swaying back and forth when I came downstairs.

I motioned to a waitress to come toward me. When she got nearer, I asked her to look up at the chandelier. She did and I asked," Is that normal?" pointing up at the chandelier.

She gradually looked up and then very sharply exclaimed, "NO!" and ran back into the diner. She did not return while I was there. This particular diner seems to have not only fine food, but fine spirits.

Chapter 7

Curse Corner

Pic taken by Chris Smith on Curse Corner. That's me in the pic with some orb visitors. The grey 1893 building is in the background.

At the corner of Fourth and Frederica, there once stood a place that few people even realize existed. I would estimate that hundreds of people drive over this intersection every single day. What they don't know is that they are driving over graves from long ago.

Owensboro was founded in1815, and it comes as no surprise to me, that at one time Fourth and

Frederica was considered the edge of town. Generally, graveyards are located at the edge of towns. If you drove over this area today, there are no tombstones to be seen. They tried to remove most of the graves and put them at Elmwood Cemetery.

I was told by Keith Lawrence, of *The Messenger Inquirer*, that not all of the graves were removed. That doesn't surprise me, because at the time of the removal, some of these graves were over a hundred years old.

In my research, I found that many single-car accidents take place on this intersection. Most of the cars crash into a tall, grey building, built in 1893. Some people claim that the cause of their crash was the fact that they saw someone or something on the intersection, and then watched it vanish. The cars swerve to dodge this *something or someone* only to look back find nothing there.

I interviewed a gentleman named Bob, from *McCarthy Towing Services,* and he told me some interesting stories. One story went like this: A lady was driving down East Fourth Street, toward the intersection, all alone. It was 2:00 a.m., which is also known as the witching or ghost hour.

She told Bob that as she approached the intersection, she saw something unexpected. All of the sudden, a man manifested and was sitting right next to her, inside her car! She swerved right and ran into the same grey building. She looked beside her and the gentleman passenger was gone.

Another story that is said to have taken place in

that same area, involved a gentleman who was approaching the intersection. Supposedly, it was also around the witching hour. He said he saw a tall gentleman in a Victorian-style suit. He was standing in the middle of the road. He swerved to dodge him and ended up hitting a pole. He looked back and saw no one.

Many times, we hear stories about this area and unusual accidents that happen there. Some say it is the ghosts of those who are buried there. They haunt the area, because of all the cars that drive over their graves. I guess I would be upset too, if someone drove over my grave every night.

Joe Ford told me an interesting story about a grave, which was close to the area that was dug up during the move. The gentleman who was digging up the grave, made a startling discovery. He noticed it looked like the grave was slightly open. So, he decided to open the crypt the remainder of the way and made a most grisly discovery. A lady had been buried alive. She had clawed the whole top of the casket. Her nails were embedded into the casket and even a tooth was found embedded into the casket.

My research found that over hundred years ago, they used to hire people to stay by the graves, in case people were accidentally buried alive. You might ask, why?

Doctors back then didn't know what a coma was, and occasionally, people would be accidentally buried alive. If they heard a sound or sensed that someone was not dead, they would dig them up, in hopes of saving them. I have found that this is the origination of the phrase we use today, "*working the graveyard shift.*"

There was also a contraption used back then, for those who might have been entombed alive. A bell would be attached to a person's toe, and a string would be brought up through a tube to where the bell was hanging. The bell was then swinging from a pole. If a person was buried alive, they could ring the bell in hopes someone would dig them up. This is where we get the term, "*dead ringer.*" It seems that our graveyards, even the ones missing tombstones, have a lot of history and perhaps some ghosts.

Chapter 8

Smith Warner Building

BeeBops

Picture taken by David Wolfe.

The Smith Warner Building was built in 1850, right before the American Civil War. If the walls could talk, what tales would they tell? This beautiful storefront plays host to several businesses and restaurants. It also hosts its fair share of haunts.

The first place of hauntings is Beebops

Pen It! Publications, LLC

Restaurant. Before it was Beebops, it was home to many types of businesses through the years. It was a notary office, a cigar emporium, where one could buy your newspaper and a good cigar. Now it is the home of the famous *BeeBop's Restaurant*.

If you love a fifties-style diner, then you will love *BeeBop's*. The atmosphere and service is to die for, no pun intended. The staff, however, see and hear a ghost!

When Samantha Cook, the owner, first opened the place she didn't know it was already occupied, by a ghost. No stories were ever told to her. She found out the hard way, when she was all alone, one morning. Sam walked into the building around 5:00 a.m. She walked in and flipped on some lights to get started with the day. She was greeted by a male voice.

It said, "Hello."

She thought at first, it was just her husband playing tricks on her. She said, "Hello," back.

There was no response to her reply. She looked around and found no one! This greeting continued a few more times, when she showed up to open the restaurant.

"It's a ghost," she told me. "We call him George."

Supposedly, if you don't answer him, weird things happen. There was a worker that came in one morning and didn't remember to greet George.

She said, "As I was leaving the back area, a pot hurled off the shelf."

She didn't know if it was thrown at her, or just thrown in anger, at her lack of greeting. Nevertheless, she was scared. She has since remembered to always say, "Hello," when entering the building.

Another incident took place, when a worker had to get something from the basement. As she was walking slowly down the staircase, she felt a cool draft. She shrugged it off to the coolness that can be found in a basement, she continued to fetch her intended item. She turned back toward the staircase, and when she looked up, she saw a shadow figure walk by and vanish into a wall.

She was quite shaken by what she had witnessed. She ran out of the basement and refused to ever go back down there.

Another waitress had an incident when she was washing dishes. When she was finished, she put her folded towel up on the shelf. She departed from the back of the building, and briefly went to the front area of the restaurant. Upon returning to the sink area, she found her towel gently folded and overlapping the two sinks. No one was back there, she claimed, which made the occurrence a bit bizarre.

The neighbors upstairs complained of hearing these phantom customers at night. One morning, Sam come in to open up the restaurant. She was confronted by the neighbors, who live upstairs.

They approached Sam and asked an odd question," Who was moving furniture and chairs last night around 3:00 a.m.?"

Puzzled, Sam looked at them and said, "No

one."

"Well someone was here, because we heard it all night long."

Sam assured them that no one was in the building and apologized for the ghostly movers.

In the back of the diner, above the last booth, there is a Photo of James Dean and Marilyn Monroe. It sits above the last booth. One day a customer and her son were sitting there, waiting on their order. A gentleman named O'Bryan brought their food and his hands were very full. O'Bryan was walking away, when out of the nowhere, the lady customer jumps and says, "OW! Why did you pinch me?"

O'Bryan looked concerned. "I did not" The customer's son even vouched for the server, saying that his hands had been full and he couldn't have pinched her.

Out of nowhere again the customer said, "OW!" Once again, she had been pinched.

Again, the server's hands were full and he was now looking at the customer quite oddly. The customers insisted to be moved to another table, immediately.

The LIG (Legends Investigating Group), whose members are, Adam Forsythe, Brad McNeal and myself, did an investigation at this diner, one night. As far as seeing anything, we did not. But, we did catch numerous EVPS. We also had a couple of personal experiences. Brad Roberts and I heard the back door opening and shutting. Keep in mind, we knew that the back door was locked.

We also caught a girl's voice, but we couldn't make out clearly what she was saying. No girl was there with us that night. It sounded like a very young girl.

The best EVP we captured, was made by a voice which came through, saying a man's name. It said out loudly and in a raspy voice," ENUS, ENUS, ENUS, ENUS, EEEEENUS!"

We let the staff hear the EVP and they were stunned, because it was so loud and clear. I could not find any Enus in my research of the building's past owners. Maybe he was a previous customer from when it was the old Cigar Emporium. It still remains a mystery to this day.

Pen It! Publications, LLC

Gambrinus

Photo taken by David Wolfe.

The Gambrinus bar has the look and feel of the bar featured in the television series, *Cheers*. It is just a very nice place to socialize. The building was erected in the 1850's, and it was once home to a variety of stores. The most interesting business was *The Louisville Dental Office*. It was this establishment for a very long time.

The first bizarre, but not necessarily ghostly story, is compliments of Jonathan, the owner of the bar. Jon said when the construction workers were in the basement of this bar doing some work, a worker accidentally knocked out one of the bricks in the chimney in the basement. What they saw amazed and startled them. All these teeth came falling out of the chimney. Apparently, the dentist had thrown old teeth down the chimney shoot to dispose of them. John says that he keeps these teeth in a jar. What a display and conversational piece it must make!

Ghosts, too, seem to want to have some fun at this bar. One day, during the remodeling period at the bar, a foreman told all his employees to go home for the evening. Everyone had left and all was quiet. Just when the foreman was about to leave, he heard someone walking from room to room upstairs. He thought he might have forgotten to tell someone to head home.

The foreman ventures slowly up the stairs, step by step. The entire time, he still hears these footsteps going from room to room. When he reached the top of the stairs, the footsteps suddenly stopped! He walked through every room, but found no one. Disturbed by what had happened, he left quickly, locking the doors behind him.

He told Rosemary Conder the story; she and her husband own the building. She had an interesting story of her own to share with him. When the building was just about done, Rosemary took her three-year-old granddaughter upstairs above the bar. It was to be the granddaughter's future home.

When they went up the stairs, the granddaughter asked her, "Grandma, who is that man standing there?"

Pen It! Publications, LLC

There was no one there. One could say it was a child's imagination, but after the stories I've heard about this bar, I doubt it.

John, the bar owner, asked me to come by one day. So, I dropped by. He wanted to show me a strange video and to tell me some about some happenings in the bar. The video he showed me was a surveillance video taken after the bar had closed.

It showed an orb, but not any ordinary orb. This orb looked like it had some intelligence to it. It was moving from the bar area to the area where the booths and seat were, almost intentionally. It acted and looked like it was almost walking around. John assured me that no air or fans were on or had been blowing. This fact made it more credible. It looked odd and was unlike any other orb I'd seen before.

During this same visit, John told me what he calls his *footstep story*. He said, "A friend was staying upstairs, all alone, one night when he heard footsteps coming down the hallway."

When John returned he told him this story. John didn't seem too surprised. John then shared with me the story of a gentleman who used to work in this building back sometime between, 2004-2005. He said this old owner claimed the place was haunted by a ghost he called "George", which is interesting because that is the same name as Sam's ghost at BeeBop's. He said that George would take things from them when they were working. Items would often just go missing. They too would hear footsteps, upstairs.

John told me that they asked a ghost hunter to

investigate the place. The ghost hunting group said the EMF detectors would go off in the basement, completely on its own. The temperature would drop in the basement in one specific area, where the EMF went off.

The last story he told me happened whenever the staff would close up at night, they would close all the lid caps on the liquor bottles. When John would come in the next morning, all the caps would be reopened. I assume the ghost patriots were not done, and wanted just one more drink for the road.

Pen It! Publications, LLC

Chapter 9

The Famous Bistro

Photo taken by David Wolfe.

The Famous Bistro building has a unique history of its own. It was built before the Civil War, but then raised in the1880's, the Famous Bistro is famous for its fine food and fine spirits, (all sorts of spirits!).

Ben Skedadis is the owner of The Famous Bistro and tells me the restaurant has a long history of ghostly events, at least while he's been in the place. Previously a second-hand toy store, Ben's family took over the building in 1992, transforming it into the current Famous Bistro.

The rumor is that the place might have once been a speakeasy, during the prohibition era. Prohibition took place during the 1920's, when the sale of alcohol was illegal. The basement of the Famous Bistro contains a hidden tunnel, which was assumed to have been a way for the speakeasy to obtain their liquor and to remain hidden from the FBI.

Owensboro has had its share of old mobsters hanging around. According to *Chicago Tribune July 7th 1946,* Bugsy Moran was arrested here in Owensboro, Ky. He was living on Littlewood Drive. So, if this was a speakeasy, one might never know who came in and out of the place, both living and dead.

Some of the tunnels were used for nothing more than a way to tunnel coal from the river. However, Ben maintains that it has a history as a speakeasy. If only the walls could tell us their tales.

The first story I'm told about this building, pertains again to it being known as a speakeasy. At one time a gentleman named, Jimmy, was a manager of this establishment. He had experiences both in the basement and on the second floor.

One particular time Jimmy threw a Christmas

party for his employees and he asked a young man to go into the basement to retrieve a bottle of wine. This young man was in the basement for only a couple minutes and came running out. He was as white as a ghost.

Jimmy tried to calm him down and to help him regain his composure. Once he finally calmed down, he told Jimmy what he had seen. This young man said he went into the basement to get the wine, and as he was bending down to get it, he looked up. He said he saw a man in a white zoot suit with outstretched arms, as though he was coming for him!

Jimmy immediately went into the basement, thinking someone might have broken in through the tunnel. He saw the same apparition, but, as the ghostly figure was coming to him, he slowly backed out of the basement. Jimmy says that, to date, the figure has not been seen again. I've often wondered if this was a customer from the speakeasy days, still looking for drink.

Jimmy has had a couple of other unique experiences in the building. One time he was giving a party on the second floor. Two girls were sitting down on a couch, enjoying the festivities, when they both noticed a little girl. She was peeking around a corner at them. The little girl then ducked back behind the corner. This happened a couple of more times, so the girls got up and went to look for the girl. However, they never found here, the little girl was gone. The girls approached Jimmy and asked him if he had any kids.

He laughed and said, "No."

They proceeded to tell him what they had seen.

He smiled and said, "Oh you're talking about my little girl ghost."

Apparently she's been spotted numerous times upstairs. Even Ben claims to have seen her standing by his bed. At the time, he had thought for some reason, that the little girl was his ex-girlfriend and yelled, "What do you want?"

When he yelled at her, the ghost covered her mouth and disappeared. I think this must be what is called an imprint, left behind from long ago. I have found no records of any little girl dying in this building. However, it could have been a customer that loved the place, when it was a toy store. She must have left an impression behind.

Some ghosts are what is called *residual ghosts*. These are the type of ghosts that can't communicate. They only appear, like a movie projector playing over and over again. That's what the girl ghost seems to do.

The first floor also had its share of odd happenings. One night, when Ben was all alone, painting the first floor, he had a strange encounter. Ben had a radio on while he was painting and was having a good time enjoying the music.

He said, "All at once, it sounded like a lot of people were talking in the room. It was quite loud."

He turned his music up louder. The phantom crowd grew louder.

Ben continued, "It sounded like a loud bar scene."

Which, if it was a speakeasy at one time,

perhaps he was hearing echoes of the past. He turned the radio up, as loud as it would go, and the phantom customers matched the volume. Ben finally turned the radio off and went home. He was done competing against the phantom customers.

The final ghost that gets a lot of attention is the, "Coughing Ghost."

Ben told me, "One time a manager, a waitress, and a cook were in the dining room. The lunch crowd had left and the place was dead (I know bad choice of words). As they were talking amongst themselves, their backs were to the front door. They heard the front door open, they heard footsteps, and then it sounded like a very rude customer was trying to get their attention. They heard a loud cough!

Naturally the waiter turned around and said, "Can I help…." not even finishing his sentence, because no one was there.

Confused, the trio looked around, but could find no one. There have been many times in the past when customers who have been sitting around the front door, would complain about a rude cough, over their shoulder. The customers would turn around to address the rude coughing diner, but no one would be there.

Ben added that even his grandfather heard this coughing ghost. His grandfather even got to see the "coughing ghost". Early one morning, Ben's grandfather was making bread, when he heard a rude customer clear his throat. He looked up and saw a man standing by the front door. The man then turned and walked through the wall!   Ben didn't seem too surprised when he heard this story either.

He said, "Nothing her has malice, things just happen."

Like I said before, the *Famous Bistro* is a place of fine food and fine spirits.

Pen It! Publications, LLC

Chapter 10

The Museum of Science and History

Pic of the Temple Theatre drawn from Lee A. Dew. Aloma Dew Owensboro The City on the Yellow Banks.

Pic above was taken by Glenda Thacker. Old Anderson's Building.

Photo of The museum of science and history. Taken by David Wolfe.

Built in the 1888, this huge building, was once home to the Temple Theatre, and is now The Museum of Science and History.

I was told by Ron Mayhue that the theatre once burned down. The legend, according to Ron, was that two actors were having an affair. The affair was discovered and they were forced to end the affair. Coincidentally, the place burned down the same night the young lovers were torn apart. Whether true or not, it does make a great, juicy story.

According to *The Owensboro City Directory*, located in the Kentucky Room at our library, in 1906 The Andersons acquired the building and turned it into Anderson's Department Store. It was the richest department store west of the Allegheny Mountains. This place was very prestigious for its day. The ladies who shopped and worked there, dressed very nice and very elaborately.

The store had three floors of merchandise and an elevator attendant to push the buttons for you. The Andersons took very good care of the place and their customers. It was a time when customer service meant giving 110%.

Mrs. Anderson was very meticulous in how she wanted the place to look and wanted the ladies in her employment to look. They were to dress very classy. Unfortunately, the store shut down in the mid 1980's.

The Museum of Science and History took over the building in the 1990's. This is where we first meet our ghost.

According to Ron Mayhue, who once worked there, three men who were working their time off for a jail sentence, had an interesting experience while in the museum.

One man told the other that he had forgotten

his tools on the second floor, in between the Wendell Ford Museum and the Kid's Playroom. So, the worker went to this area and found his tools. As he bent down, he slowly looked up to find a boy standing in front of him. The boy wore an old Irish cap, knickers, and a haversack. The boy looked at him, smiled and ran right through the wall!

The gentleman yelled and ran to relay his experience to his friends. Of course, they found nothing there, when they went back.

One place we find that the little boy loves to play is in the Playseum, in the Shadow Room. This room has phosphor in the walls and a flash button. When you press the button, it flashes and your shadow is displayed on the wall for several seconds. Ron was giving a personal tour to a lady and her daughter. They got to the Playseum and Ron said he needed to run an errand on the other side of the Museum.

He told them, "Check out the Shadow Room. It's fun."

The ladies went into the Shadow Room to play. They spread out like gingerbread men. Mom was right next to her daughter, with their arms and legs spread out. They pressed the button and, after it flashed, there was the mom's shadow, the daughter's shadow, and then a shadow of a little boy. They were most perplexed over this, but must have figured it was part of the fun. When they saw Ron later on, they questioned him about it. He assured them he had nothing to do with it.

The little boy has been spotted numerous times

in the Playseum. One person even caught him in a photograph.

A lady was in the room with her daughter and they were playing, all by themselves. She took a Photo of her daughter in one of the tubes, and low and behold, there was a little boy standing beside her daughter. She assured me that no one else was in that room. It frightened her when she saw this little boy standing beside her daughter.

There have been times, on my tour, that we've seen the room flash, all by itself. My customers pointed it out! If you're outside of the museum and look up to the second floor window, on the right side, you will see it. There is a dark covering over the window. Perhaps, you will see the flash in the window, long after the museum has closed for the evening.

Photo taken from a customer on my tour. She was all alone in

this room. To the right in the circle is a little boy

Little boy in the circle taken by a customer.

Pen It! Publications, LLC

Pic taken by Chris Smith two little boys with an orb friend to the left of them.

Other areas of the museum have their share of strange stories. Ron told me that the Wendell Ford Museum, is one of those areas.

One morning Ron was making his rounds and he entered into the Wendell Ford part of the museum. There is section that has a barber shop scene in which one mannequin has on a baseball cap, and the other does not.

When Ron got to that area, he noticed something wasn't right. The baseball cap was missing. He approached a coworker and told them what he had seen. Together, they went back to the area and the baseball cap had re-appeared, but it was on the other mannequin head. Ron couldn't explain it!

In the same barbershop scene, there is a hot

mask on a mannequin's face. On numerous occasions, this hot mask would be off the face when workers would make their rounds in the morning. They would return it to its rightful spot and the next morning, it would be on the floor again.

I was told by workers, that faucets would turn on in restrooms and paper towels would be pulled from the dispenser.

The best story Ron told me about was when Cris, a manager, was by himself on the third floor. This floor contains a picture of Mr. and Mrs. Anderson. One night, he brought his little dog with him to work. This little dog is very docile and doesn't bark at anything. While Cris was on the third floor, he gave the dog free reign to look around. He heard his dog start to growl and bark at something. So, he went out to find him. He found the dog in front of Mrs. Anderson's picture, barking and growling viciously. The dog suddenly relieved itself. I don't mean just urinate, I mean really relieved itself!

When Ron heard about this, he brought his dog in and it did the same thing again. It barked and growled at Mrs. Anderson's picture and then relieved itself. I was told three dogs have done this near the area where the picture is located. Apparently no dog likes this picture, or perhaps Mrs. Anderson wasn't a dog lover!

The museum had *a* hypnotist, Kathleen Peters, come in and she supposedly allowed spirits to come in through her body. She said the first spirit that came in was Mrs. Anderson. Mrs. Anderson conveyed to her displeasure that the building is now a museum and that she wanted it converted back into her beloved department store. She talked about how she wanted her female employees dressed. One could tell that she was definitely in charge.

Another spirit that came through, was that of the little boy from the Playseum. He claimed that he died in a fire in 1890's. Which was when the building had supposedly burned. Coincidence, maybe, maybe not. It's not what I believe, but what you believe that matters.

Chapter 11

River Park Center

River Park center pic by David Wolfe.

When you look at the RiverPark Center and The Bluegrass Museum, one might say that they look fairly new. I can tell you for certain that they are fairly haunted.

According to the *River Park Center* website, The RiverPark Center construction began in 1991 and it opened for business in 1992. Before it was opened, I noticed in some old pictures, that there was once a huge building on the property, and then at one time, it was just bare land.

Pen It! Publications, LLC

Legend has it that a lady committed suicide, by jumping into the river, around the turn of the century. Again. this is just a legend, but it seems to follow along with our stories.

It was in the evening time, in 1996, on the side stage area. Todd Reynolds, Debbie Reynolds (his wife), and some actors were getting ready to go on stage for a play which Todd was directing. (Todd is a person whose name we hear a lot in this chapter. He is a person who has had a lot of encounters with ghosts.) As they were getting ready to go on stage, Debbie and the stage manager, Troy Lot, noticed a lady walking on a grid above them. They said she was in white and was walking south to north on the grid. Troy was behind the curtains and Debbie was looking up at the stage, both in separate areas. They were quite startled at their sighting. One wonders if this was our legendary suicide ghost.

But, the story doesn't end there. During the run of the same play, but on a different night, the play was going according to plan. The spotlight shined on actress, Ann Welsh. Todd was up in his booth and noticed something out of the normal. Todd noticed a spotlight shining on a chair. As this light shined on this chair, a shadow passed across the light. It looked as though someone walked in mid-air, in front of it. There was no way this could've happened. A bit perplexed, Todd went to the booth to check for an explanation concerning what he had just seen. But, as soon as the light appeared, it vanished. Maybe the ghost was putting on an impromptu performance of its own.

Another occurrence involving Todd, happened one night, just as he was leaving the RiverPark Center, with Todd Ruth Barrett and Star Waddell.   At this point, Todd had worked there 13 years, as the tech director. They closed up and proceeded to exit the building. As they were walking towards the front door, they heard in the distance, the sound of a door latch.

When they reached the source of the sound, they made a startling discovery. On the second floor, above the reception area, there is a door leading into Cannon Hall. This door has a long door knob that requires you to pull it down to open the door. As they approached the door, they all stared in disbelief as the doorknob rattled on its own. It appeared as though someone was locked in and was trying to exit from the other side. Todd knew that there was no knob on the other side of the door.

One lady said, "Todd, it looks like someone's locked in on the other side of the door."

Todd said, "That's impossible. No one's here except us. Besides," he said. "It's rattling on our side.   It's one of those door knobs that opens from one side only."

The girls were shaken up and ready to leave, at that point.

I asked Todd if he opened the door. He laughed and said, "Yeah, the next day."

Another interesting story Todd tells of the very haunted River Park Center, occurred as he was setting up some eight-foot tables with sheets for the play, *Tops*.

Pen It! Publications, LLC

Todd had freshly laundered the sheets and retrieved them from the laundry area. As he began to put them on the tables, one of the edges folded in on one of the corners.

"No big deal," he thought. Then, the sheet unfolded itself from the corner! It was as if someone had grabbed the end of it to help him unfold it and pull it straight. Todd said," Thank you," and left.

I'm one of those people who would not want to hear a ghost say my name. I have experienced this just once and did not enjoy the experience. Todd has had that very same thing happen to him.

He carries a walkie talkie radio with him at all times, and it beeps if the batteries are running low. One night, the radio was beeping, so Todd sat it on a chair until he could replace the batteries. Then, Todd said, the radio crackled and a voice came through,

"Todd," it said.

He figured he had forgotten to turn it off and moved to turn the power knob to the offsetting, but it was already off. Thinking logically, he assumed that a co-worker had called his name. He located Dean and asked him if he had called his name. Dean replied that he hadn't called for him.

Thinking that Dean was pulling a prank on him, Todd looked at the other workers and asked, "Is he lying to me?"

When they all replied no, Todd left the room both puzzled and a little spooked.

Todd told me that Troy had a similar incident. Troy was sitting in his office, around 2:00 a.m., naturally, he was all alone. Out of nowhere, he heard a voice say, "Troyyyyyy!!!" Troy left suddenly and never worked nights again.

Voices and apparitions aren't the only unusual happenings in this big beautiful building. Phantom footsteps are also often heard throughout the building.

Jim was out driving with his wife, Marsha. Jim worked at the RiverPark Center and needed to make a phone call, so he stopped by the Center to use the phone. Jim went to his office to make the call, knowing that he was the only one in the building. As he picked up the phone, he heard a door open and footsteps come down the hall toward his office. He waited, thinking someone would walk by, but no one did. He peaked out of the office to look for the visitor, but no one was there. Jim decided his phone call could wait and hurriedly exited the building.

Another friend of mine, Ann Welsh, is an actress/costume designer for the RiverPark Center. Ann's had a couple of experiences of her own. In the mid 1990's, Mrs. Ann was working on a play called *Summer Shorts.*

Her story is as follows: "We were performing on the Cannon Hall Stage and I had a rehearsal. Debbie was there for another rehearsal and it was just the two of us sitting on the sofa on the stage, talking. On the stage, the work lights were shining. All of the sudden, a light on one of the battens came on. However, the battens were unplugged! Naturally, we both left in quite a hurry."

I guess the ghost thought they were ready to

perform.

Another story Ann told me, connects us with one of the stories Todd told me.

Ann said, "Todd and Debbie was directing a play. Whenever an actor is on stage, they can always can feel the light. I knew I was in the light and then, suddenly I wasn't! At that time Todd and Debbie saw the light go off and looked up to see a hazy, white shape, flowing in front of the lighting equipment."

I would assume this is what is known as, our torso ghost. In the past, others have relayed similar encounters with the mysterious lady in white.

The International BlueGrass Museum

Above: Photos taken by David Wolfe outside and inside of the Bluegrass museum.

Our Bluegrass Museum has had its share of haunts too, as it is connected to the Riverpark Center. Apparently, our lady ghost has no barriers that prevent her from moving between the two.

The Bluegrass Museum was built back around the same time as the River Park Center. Around 100 years ago, it was an agi store for almost 60 years. In the mid 1990's, it became the Bluegrass Museum.

This story takes place back in 2010, when a horrible storm hit the downtown area. Lightning was striking everywhere and the power outages were numerous. Of course, this is the perfect setup for a ghost story.

Pen It! Publications, LLC

During the storm, the alarm was triggered at the Bluegrass Museum and two police officers were dispatched to investigate. The officers arrived at the location before the key holder showed up to unlock the doors. When she showed up, things started to get a little weird. The key holder went out of her car and started mumbling to herself, "This is not right, this is not right, this is not right!"

The two police officers looked at each other, as if to say, "Did you hear that?"

They simply shrugged it off and went inside. The officers were very thorough, going through every floor and found all to be calm.

They asked her, "Is this all?"

She said, "No, I have to go through a door into a room. If the door shuts I will have to go through the whole museum…. in the dark…. alone."

While the key holder went to reset the alarm, the police officers stood by the door. As the officers waited, they heard someone going up the stairwell to the second floor. They heard the second floor door open and then shut. Then they heard someone running upstairs. This made the officers uneasy and put them on guard. Suddenly, the key holder walked out of the door and completely surprised the officers.

They asked her, "Did you go upstairs?"

She said, "No, you saw me. I went into that room!"

As the officers were arguing with her the elevator began to move. They asked the key holder," Is this one of the elevators that goes on and off by itself."

She said, "No, you have to push the button for the floor you are visiting."

It was coming to their floor, the first floor. Thinking their perpetrator was on that elevator, the police officers tensed, weapons drawn. The elevator descended to the first floor and then the door opened......no one was there.

But, that's not where the story ends. They asked the key holder if there was a surveillance room.

She said, "Yes, but you'll have to go down this long hallway."

The officers walked down the hallway and entered the surveillance room. As they were reviewing the footage, one officer pointed to the screen and asked, "Wait! Did you see that?"

They both watched, as a shadowy figure moved across the screen. They then saw footage of themselves, walking down the hallway. Beside them walked a black, shadowy figure that followed them the entire way. As they entered the surveillance room, the figure entered with them. The police officers thanked the key holder for being so cooperative and retreated quickly back to the police station.

One of the officers was Officer Youngman. He is also a Gulf War Veteran and never believed in ghosts, until this experience. He has not been back to the building since this incident and has no plans to visit anytime soon.

Pen It! Publications, LLC

The Crème'

Photo above taken by David Wolfe.

Photo above taken by David Wolfe.

Pen It! Publications, LLC

The building that now houses The Crème', was built in 1881 by the Wile Brothers. It has been a lot of different stores throughout its life.

According to The Owensboro directory in the Kentucky Room, from 1886 to 1893, it was home to Loddie HF & Wm Music Instruments. This is an interesting back story, as they now hold live music shows at The 'Crème'.

It was also once a jewelry store, drug store, clothing store, antique store, and then, finally, The Crème'. The Conders bought the building in 2006 and completely renovated it. This family has done a great job renovating and rebuilding our downtown area and are credited with saving many buildings.

I guess the ghosts also owe them a debt of gratitude. By saving these old buildings, the ghosts still have a place to haunt.

The downstairs of the coffee house has never had any problems with ghosts, but the upstairs is a whole different story. In my opinion, the upstairs has so many stories they could make a movie or write a book, just on it alone.

Terri was once a tenant in the upstairs apartment. She had problems with a ghost who loved to walk upstairs at night.

One night, not long after she moved in, she awoke to the sound of the front door opening and shutting. SLAM! Then she heard this intruder walk up the steps, slowly, one step at a time. Then the footsteps walked over into the living room and something sat down on her couch. Her apartment is a studio apartment, so as soon whatever it was sat down on the couch, she flipped on the light. Nothing was there and the sounds instantly stopped. The only sound she heard was her heart beating rapidly.

When Terri finally moved out of the upstairs apartment, she decided to take one last picture of the place, so she took a photograph. When she downloaded the picture to her computer, she was amazed by what she saw.

There was a man looking back at her through the glass foyer. Terri sent me the picture herself and I must admit it does look compelling. She assured me that man was not there when she took the picture.

Shawna moved into the apartment after Terri, and she also experience the phantom footsteps phenomenon. But, things got worse, for her. In an interview with Shawna, on April 6th, 2010, she told me many stories about the hauntings.

She had heard footsteps, but she said one day she was on the floor playing with her son. Out of nowhere, she heard her son's baby rattler rattle. He was not playing with it, and there were no vehicles traveling by that could have caused a vibration to cause it to rattle on its own. It was just sitting in the floor rattling.

Another time, Shawna was sitting in the dining room when, out of nowhere, she got a chill. It was as though a presence went through the room and she said the air around her almost felt electric.

She also said that her baby would wave at someone standing there when there was no one else in the room. Many times she would come home and the bathroom door would be shut, when she knew that she left it open.

The area in the back is where things would always happen. One day, she was in the kitchen and she had a remote control sitting on a table. In an instant, it flew off the table and crashed to the floor!

She to acknowledge whatever it was. She said, "I don't know who you are, but you're going to have to tell me."

She told me, "It knocks things around to get attention."

One night, Shawna and her boyfriend were watching TV. They heard a loud boom! They thought the cat knocked something off a table again, as it had done before. When they looked down, they saw the cat laying on the floor beside them.

They went to investigate and found that the humidifier had fallen over of its own accord. This was a pretty heavy item and would require some force to knock it over.

My favorite story is the one about the "shadow man". Around the holidays, she and her boyfriend were getting ready for a holiday function.

As her boyfriend went to the back area of the closet, he stopped and asked, "Did you just walk back there to the closet?"

She replied, "No, I've been right putting my shoes on."

He felt as though he was being watched. He looked over and whatever was there was moving fast.

When he looked at it, the figure was startled and ran through the wall.

Shawna said she saw the shadow man on another occasion, in the closet area. Once again, he walked right through the wall.

Her boyfriend, Mitchell, was alone one day and he heard something. He looked up to see a spice bottle just rolling across the floor, all by itself. He thought about the cat, but again, the cat right beside him.

Shawna has seen doors open by themselves. On several occasions she has detected the smell of cologne. Next door at The Crowne, Becky has also experienced the smell of cologne. Which will lead to our next story.

Pen It! Publications, LLC

The Crowne

Photo taken by David Wolfe.

The Crowne was built around the same time as The Crème' Coffee House, in the 1800's, and was also built by the Wile Brothers. It too has been a variety of stores over the years.

Before the Conders bought the building, Bob Puckett owned it. According to the *Owensboro Living* website, "The Conders purchased the building, which was constructed circa 1887, in 2006.

According to Rosemary Conder, the beautiful old structure was saved from ruin by the late Bob Puckett. In fact, the Conders named the building "The Crowne" in Puckett's honor. Bob had a passion for antiques and entertaining, and used the building to showcase both! We hear he often was referred to as 'the King' and there is crown decor throughout the building!"

Apparently The King didn't want to leave his throne, even after death. In fact, the ghost that haunts the place is named Bob, after Bob Puckett.

Becky, who used to work at the Crowne, had the most encounters of anyone I spoke with. I remember talking to the young girl who was working at the Crème'. She told me her job was to clean The Crowne late at night, and she was always by herself. She said that she never quite felt comfortable in the room, known as the Honeymoon Suite. She said she always felt like she was being watched.

When I told Becky the young girl's story, she said, "That's nothing, I had my experience in that same room."

A young couple wanted to rent the room for a night. Becky went upstairs to clean and prepare the room for guests. She made her way through the room and, while making her rounds, closed the toilet lid and left the bathroom door open. When Becky led the couple into their room, she stopped and stared at what greeted her.

Pen It! Publications, LLC

She told me, "David, the bathroom door was closed. Upon opening the door, I noted the toilet lid was up."

I guess even in the afterlife you still get the urge to "go". It was most likely a male ghost because, let's be honest, us guys keep the lid up. Right ladies?

Becky had other experiences, as well. She indicated that she even though the ghost may have followed her home one night. One evening, after her shift, she went home and, as the hour grew late, Becky went to bed. During the night, she had a feeling of being watched. She looked up and saw a figure standing there, watching her and her husband sleep. I guess Bob was so fond of Becky, that he followed her home. Becky stated that she never had any encounters with ghosts until she worked at The Crowne.

One winter's day Becky and her son were at the front of the store doing some work. She heard the door open in the back, then some footsteps, and then the door opened again. This happened several times throughout the day. She briefly thought maybe it was her son going in and out of the store. But, she sometimes when it happened, he was right there with her.

Her son looked up at her and said, "Momma, I heard those steps too."

Perhaps Bob was just saying, "Hello".

Becky said she also experienced the usual cold spots and other feelings of being watched. But, the event that she relates most to, occurred when Becky announced she was leaving The Crowne. As soon as she made the announcement, the grand chandelier came crashing down!

Becky said, "I guess Bob didn't take my news very well."

Pen It! Publications, LLC

Chapter 13

The Old Trinity Church
aka. the Theatre Workshop

Photo taken by David Wolfe.

Haunts of Owensboro

Photo taken by David Wolfe. Note the strange orb on top of the building.

According to the *Owensboro Directory,* located in the Owensboro Library Kentucky Room, *Trinity Center for Theatre Workshop* was built in 1875. It is one of the oldest Gothic architectural-style churches in Western Kentucky and we are lucky to have it in Owensboro, Kentucky.

Until 1963, It was an Episcopal Church. Then it became the Cliff Hagan Boys and Girls Club. In 1973, the Theatre Workshop of Owensboro acquired the building and has been housed there since that time.

Other than the great theatrical performances that have been given throughout the years, the ghosts seem to like putting on their own performances. These ghostly performances are given both inside and outside the building. This building is reportedly one of the most haunted spots in the tri-state area surrounding Owensboro, Kentucky.

I have had a couple of experiences in this location and can attest to the statements that follow.

The legend of why this place is so haunted begins in the 1890's. The legend goes, that a priest had a daughter around the age of thirteen or fourteen. Many people look at me oddly when I say a priest had a daughter, but Episcopalian priests are allowed to marry.

His daughter approached him one particular night and told him about the man she had fallen in love with, and intended to marry. The priest knew her intended and had heard reports of the gentleman's questionable reputation. He told his daughter that she would absolutely not marry him. He refused to have the man in his home or in his church. He forbade her to ever see her beau again.

The daughter dropped the subject and appeared to comply with her father's order. However, a few weeks later, the daughter again approaches her father with some news. She had gone against her father's wishes and she is now pregnant.

Her father flew into a rage and called her some horrible names. He kicked her out of his house and declared that she was dead to him! Obviously, the daughter was greatly distressed by her father's actions. She ascended the bell tower and hung herself.

The next morning, the priest entered the front door and saw his daughter hanging from the bell tower. He realized that he had driven her to take her life, so the priest goes into the basement and book his own life, which is a mortal sin. Since then, this place has been very haunted.

One Halloween night, a Medium visited the theater, with my tour crowd.   This medium said that two ghosts were there and the gentleman's name was George and the daughter's name was Elizabeth.

Other questions about this tale arose when a ghost-hunting group visited the establishment. On an EVP, when the gentleman ghost hunter asked Elizabeth, "Did you take your life?" she quite clearly replied, "No. Murder."

I will go on record and say I have researched this building and its history, quite thoroughly, and have never found any mention of a murder in the building. It's just a mystery that may never be solved.

Another story that has been passed down through the years, involves another priest found dead in the basement. Some say that either he took his life in the front basement, or he slipped and fell down the stairs. I believe that if the story is true, he probably accidentally fell down the steps.   They are quite steep.

The reason for the mention of that story is because it leads into a present day story.   One day, a pest control agent named, Doug, was down in the front basement. Other than Doug, there was only one other person in the building, Mike, the Director. As Doug was spraying for insects, the basement suddenly went black.

Pen It! Publications, LLC

When the lights are off in the basement, it is so dark that you can barely see your hand in front of your face. You can imagine the level of fear that Doug experienced. The lights turned back on, only to be turned off again. This happened several times.

Doug's fear turned into anger, that someone was playing such a trick on him. He stormed upstairs and heads all the way back to where Mike is working and yells, "Why do you keep turning the lights on and off?"

Mike said, "Sir, I was never up front. I've been in the back the entire time."

Doug questioned, "You were never up front at all?"

Mike replied, "No!"

Doug then shook Mike's hand and said, "Thank you very much, have a good day".

He quickly went out the front door and never returned.

A strange death that is rumored to have happened, came to light during a lock-in with a group of teenage girls. Cris Hart was chaperoning the lock-in, and one of the girls had brought an Ouija board. (It should be noted that I will not touch an Ouija board. I believe that you may get a visitor that you cannot get rid of.)

The odd thing is, none of the girls were brave enough to even touch it.

So Cris said, "I'll do it". During an interview, Cris told me that once she agreed to touch the board, she felt an electric jolt run up her arm. She asked a question before putting her fingers on the board, "Did you die here?"

The pendulum moved on its own to the word yes. Keep in mind her fingers were not even on the board yet. As she put her fingers on the board, she asked, "How did you die?" It spelled the word, *drowning*.

She was perplexed, "Drowning? How?" She asked its name. *Victor*. She went back to the drowning question, because she was still puzzled over it.

"How did you drown?"
Baptismal pool.

Then, things got really strange. A chandelier suddenly came crashing down!

The house manager at the time, came out and said, "Take that thing out of here and never bring it back!"

When the board went out the door the activity stopped. It appears that they might have at least four ghosts in this building. According to a Medium, there are four to five spirits.

The gentleman who has had the best experiences, is Todd Reynolds. A name we previously referred to in my Riverpark chapter. Todd has been involved in the TWO for over 40 years, as an actor, a director, producer, and more. Since Todd has lots of ghostly experiences, it seems that the ghosts may like him or perhaps he is just open to the experiences.

Let me tell you a story that has been relayed to me by two separate witnesses, Todd Reynolds and Ann

Welsh. Todd, Ann, Debbie Reynolds, Ken Butler, Ed Dupont, and Julia Jennings were sitting around after rehearsal and talking. Suddenly, the back door opened. They knew that the door was locked, so Todd though someone had unlocked it and was getting ready to walk inside. There was no one visible. The "visitor" apparently walked over to the basement door and slammed it shut!

Todd looked at the others and asked, "Did you see that?"

The other actors just nodded silently and appeared to be in a state of shock. They continued their previous conversation and tried to ignore what they had just witnessed.

About five minutes later, their "visitor" walked back up the steps, reopened the basement door, slammed it shut, walked over to the back door, exited and slammed the back door.

Todd looking at his watch said, "Well it's time to go home."

One Saturday, in 1993, Todd was in the TWO by himself, working on a set for the play *Cemetery Club*. Todd had his plans laid out on a table, along with his tape measure. He went to get some supplies and when he returned to the table, he noticed that his tape measure was gone. Thinking maybe he had moved it, he began to look for it.

After searching for several minutes, he finally walked up towards the stage and said, "Ok, Sid, Fred, George, did you take my tape measure?"

Todd stepped back toward the table, and the

tape measure was there on the table, exactly where he had left it. Perhaps George needed the tool for a while, and then replaced it. Or maybe this was a prank from our little ghost, Victor. It sounded like something a child would do.

In 2002, Todd was sponsoring a summer youth program about acting. He was on the stage with approximately 40 kids. He was walking back and forth on the stage and he said that he saw a lone girl sitting about two or three rows back. She looked to be about the age of 13, had dark, straight hair and was wearing a dress. This girl was just intently staring at Todd. It gave him an odd feeling.

Todd had heard no one else come in the building and all the students were on stage. He told me, "The students never mentioned her."

As he walked stage left and then turned to stage right, he looked out to where the girl sat. She had vanished. Could this be the ghostly image of Elizabeth that Todd saw?

The last story that Todd shared with me, happened in 2006. It is one of the best and oddest occurrences on record. Todd was all alone during the day inside the TWO, waiting for a local florist to make a delivery for the set. He was sitting down and leaning back against the rail of a walkway. He heard some footsteps coming out of the green room. The footsteps proceeded down the hall and then cut over to enter onto the stage.

Todd is a very rational person, and thought that perhaps someone was in the back of the theater. So he yelled, "Hello? Hello? Hello?" No received no response, other than footsteps sounding on the stage. Todd then asked, "Okay, are you an old friend that has passed on?" He individually called their names and then asked, "Are you the one that opened the door and took my tape measure?"

Then, out of the corner of his eye, he saw something that both startled and amazed him. Todd saw this big orb hovering above the stage. It was a big ball of light and Todd described it as reminding him of Glenda's bubble from *The Wizard of Oz*. The orb grew until it reached the size of a soccer ball and then it moved toward the auditorium. When it reached the window, it dissolved into tiny bubbles resembling an Alka Seltzer tablet placed into water.

Todd said the room was full of energy and he couldn't move. Todd asked, "Ok I saw that. Can you do it again?"

Down the middle aisle, where all the chairs were pulled out, he heard three or four footsteps and then the sound faded away. This is the most bizarre occurrence that I've ever heard about. This orb wasn't like the ones that I've photographed, it was fully round and seemed to have its own energy source.

Others who have worked or volunteered there, also have their own ghost stories to share.

Cris Hart's husband said he was working alone one night, in the sound booth. He heard footsteps walk up the stairs, across the floor to the sound booth, and then walk directly behind him. He looked over his left shoulder and saw a shadow figure standing behind him. Without hesitation, Mr. Hart abruptly left. Since then, he says that he always knocks on the banister before going upstairs.

I had a painter call me one day to tell me about an experience he had back in the 1970's. He said he was painting the place one day and decided to take a lunch break. Before he left, he placed his paint bucket on the scaffold. When he returned from lunch, the bucket was gone. Confused, he began to look for it. Finally, he walked back to the green room and found it sitting the middle of the floor. This took place three different times. Knowing that there was no one else in the building, the painter was a little baffled. Upon entering the room to claim his paint bucket, he heard a disembodied voice say, "Don't do it!" The painter left the building that day both perplexed at the events that had unfolded and more than a little spooked.

A young actress named Alexis Roberts also had an experience in the green room, late one night. Like any good ghost story, this one happened on a dark, stormy night, when Lexi was all alone in the green room.

She was in between sets of a play and was texting while she waited. She heard a loud clap of thunder and then the back door opened and shut by itself. Lexi thought nothing of it and attributed the occurrence to the wind. She got up to make sure the door was shut and closed tight so that it would not happen again. The lightning flashed and a loud clap of thunder sounded again. The door opened and closed again, but this time there was an added feature. The ghost walked to the fuse panel box and opened the door and then shut it.

Lexi said, "Okay," and ran to the front of the building.

I have had a couple of incidences at TWO. But, there have been others who have either been on my tour or investigated the TWO and witnessed their own ghostly performances.

One winter day, I was leading a ghost tour, and we were in the back area, outside by the back door. This is the same door that had opened by itself, in the past. I told them all the stories and then I asked one girl if she would like to use my EMF detector. She said that she would like to and took the device and sat close to the door.

As she is sitting there, her friend begins to take lots of pictures with her rather expensive-looking camera. This camera had a very large lens and she was able to take frame by frame shots. As the girl's friend snapped her picture, the EMF detector lit up. I encouraged her to remain still and to keep holding it steady.

Then her friend who was taking the pictures said," Oh my gosh! Oh my gosh! Oh my gosh!" She screamed and ran off my tour. To this day, she's the only person to ever run away from my tour.

I went after her and I asked her to return. She did so, reluctantly, and she showed me what had frightened her. She had captured a photo of a white figure coming out of the wall and turning into a large, white ball of ectoplasm mist.

We were all a little spooked after that night.

Photo taken by a tourist. This is the ghost that came out of the wall.

Pen It! Publications, LLC

Picture taken by my niece, Heather Howard

Photo taken by a tourist in October of 2015. No one was in the area. Very weird!

Photo above taken by David Wolfe.

Another occurrence happened right outside that same door. I was with my niece, Heather, and she was taking promotional pictures for my website. Suddenly, we heard footsteps walking behind us. They sounded as though someone was shuffling through the gravel.

My niece said, "Uncle David, did you hear that?"

I said, "Quick! Take a picture." She did, and managed to capture a picture of the same ectoplasm ball that the tourist had captured with her camera. I also snapped a photo of a shadowy figure by the back area, that we call the Cowboy Ghost. I've took two pictures of what looks like a shadow figure wearing big, ten-gallon hat.

The best experience that ever happened to me, was when I was investigating with a group out of Vine Grove, KY. The group is called P.A.S.T. They are quite famous, in their own right, having helping groups like T.A.P.S. and Patti Starr with investigations.

Our investigation time was the opposite of most paranormal groups, as we were investigating during the early morning hours up until about noon. I'm glad we did so, because we caught more during the day than we ever did at night. In fact, most experiences happen there during the day.

As we were investigating, we went back to the costume closet which contains a chair called the "ghost chair." Supposedly, a gentleman died while sitting in this chair and since then, there has been ghostly activity. I was there with one of the founder's, Stan Howard's wife, Julie.

I'm a very impatient person and ghost hunting is often like fishing; you may not always get a bite or that big fish. Therefore, I am not the best fisherman, nor am I the best ghost hunter.

We were standing around, and my impatience got the best of me. I said, "If there's something here, make one of these costumes move."

It was a stupid statement, but apparently it was the right thing to say. All the EMF detectors lit up and then about ten footsteps sounded behind me and entered the green room.

Julie said, "Dave, did you do that?"

I said, "Absolutely not! You're looking at me

and I'm standing still."

We decided it was time to move on. During that investigation, we caught about ten EVPS, which were great! One voice even whispered," David" in creepy voice. I was really bothered by that one.

We caught an EVP that sounded like a choir chanting. We clearly heard them say "Thine House!" along with some other words, we couldn't quite make out. This leads into my next story.

Todd Reynolds told me a story about two girls who were coming to the TWO one night to drop off some clothing. As they approached the front door, they heard something out of the ordinary, a choir singing, loudly. They knew that no one else was supposed to be in the building.

The girls opened the door, and the choir's song got louder. As they stepped over the threshold, the sound stopped, abruptly. The girls screamed and threw all the clothing inside building and left quickly.

I have interviewed others, who worked inside the building, who claim to have also heard this ghostly choir.

My final story involves the time I managed to capture a full-bodied apparition with my camera. I was helping to pack up our gear after a tour, and I grabbed the camera and said, "I'm going to take one more picture." As I said this, our Ovilus turned on and said three very disturbing words, "Demon! Demon! Demon!"

At the time, I didn't know that I had captured anything with my camera.

Pen It! Publications, LLC

Julie called me that night and asked me if I checked my email. I said, "No, why?"

She informed me that we had captured the holy grail of ghost pictures. I went home after my tour, checked my email, and found out that she was right. There was a demonic looking figure standing there.

Many people have looked at this picture and shuddered. I love the looks on their faces when I show it to my tour visitors. I can't say it was a demon, in fact, I like to think it's not! Maybe it was just George or someone else's reflection from the past. I can honestly say because of my own experiences, the TWO is one of the most haunted places I've ever heard of and I'll put it up against many other famous places that are haunted.

I challenge you go there see a great play and see if you too will be entertained by more than just the actors.

Photo above taken by David Wolfe and P.A.S.T This is the demon of TWO.

Pen It! Publications, LLC

Photo taken by David Wolfe and P.A.S.T.

Photo taken by a tourist. It was dark and no one was in front of the stage but me. 2014

Pen It! Publications, LLC

Photo taken by David Wolfe.

The Final Chapter

I have thoroughly enjoyed writing this book. I never thought I would ever write a book. I'm not a writer, I'm a Storyteller/Entertainer.

I have to thank all those who helped me with stories, interviews, and research. If you believe in ghosts after reading this book, great! If you don't, then that's fine too!

Why would I say that? Well if I entertained you, then I have done my job.

I'll end here with one final question; do you know where the world's first ghost story came from? Give up? The Bible. Be sure to check out first Samuel, Chapter 28. It contains a witch, a ghost, and a king. It's a great story. I invite you to read it and share it with your kids. Trust me, they will love it!

Pen It! Publications, LLC

Bibliography

Chapter 1
Website: *http://www.findagrave.com/.*
https://tshaonline.org/handbook/online/articles/fsm5
5.
www.findagrave.com
Interview with Joe Ford about Last public hanging,
March 30th, 2005.
http://murderpedia.org/male.B/b/bethea-rainey-
photos.htm.

Chapter 2.
Interview with security guards at *Executive Inn*, January
12th, 2005.
Interview with Josh, the last security guard in Big E,
April, 20th, 2009.
Prostitution folder in KY Room Library.
Evansville Courier and Press website.
Interview with Judge Lanham, Oct, 30th, 2007.
Interview with Big E Desk Clerk, September 1st, 2007.
Interview with Big E Manager, September 1st, 2007.
Topix website story about big E ghost.

Chapter 3
The Messenger Inquirer, 2002
Newspaper, *The Monitor.*
60 years of Owensboro William Potter Hayes 1883-
1943.
Interview with a barge worker March 12th, 2006.
Customer interview, May, 2012.

Chapter 4:
Book: *Ladies of Civil War Owensboro* in *Kentucky Room,* Owensboro Public Library.
HOODOO, CONJURE, and ROOTWORK; AFRICAN AMERICAN FOLK MAGIC by Catherine Yronwode.
60 years of Owensboro by William Potter Hayes, 1883-1943.
Interview with Mrs. P, May, 2006.

Chapter 5:
Owensboro Directory, in Kentucky Room Library, Courthouse records.
Records in Kentucky Room, *Last Public Hanging* folder.
Interview with Tim Hopkins, June 12th, 2004.
Interview with Stephen Hopkins, June 12th, 2004.
Interview with Mr. Dixon, May, 16th, 2007.
Records at the Haley McGinnis Funeral home, Website address:
http://www.haleymcginnis.com/who-we-are/history-and-staff.
Interview with Shirlene, coworker at *The Haley McGinnis*, September 8, 2013.
Records located at *The Campbell Club.*
Waitress interview, (Name omitted) July, 2010.
Interview with Matt Weafer, September 20th, 2015.
Miller House website add the website address here.
The Messenger Inquirer.
Interview with Mrs. Kirk, September 20th, 2011.
Interview with Arron King, September 23rd, 2011.
Chapter 6:

Interview with Naomi, March 15th, 2012.
Interview with Bill and Staff, September 15, 2014-2015.

Chapter 7:
Interview with Keith Lawrence, August 15th, 2006.
1883 History of Daviess County, Kentucky., where is this info located??
Interview with Bob, from McCarty's Towing, August 20th, 2006.
Joe Ford's Book on ghost and interview, name of book and date of the interview here.

Chapter 8:
Interview with Samantha Ellison, September 12, 2013.
Interview with O'Bryan, September, 2015 and May, 2016.
Interview with Jonathan, Owner of *Gambrinus Pub.*
Interview with Rosemary Conder, September, 2006.

Chapter 9:
Interview with Ben, he owner, September, 2006.
Chicago Tribune, July 7th, 1946.
Interview with Jimmy, previous manager, 2006.

Chapter 10:
Interview with Ron Mayhue, July, 2006.
Owensboro City Directory, in the Kentucky Room at the Owensboro Public Library.
Interview with tour customer, 2010.
Interview with Katherine Peters, 2010.

Chapter 11:
River Park Center website, add web address here.
Interview with Todd Reynolds, Sept 1st, 2006.
Interview with Ann Welsh, 2006.
Interview with Debbie Reynolds, 2006.
Interview with Officer Youngman, 2011.
Interview with Todd Reynolds, May 24th, 2016.

Chapter 12:
The courthouse record, in the basement of the courthouse.
Interview with Shawna, 2010.
Interview with Becky, previous manager of The Crown, date here.
Owensboro Living website.

Chapter 13:
Owensboro Library Kentucky Room, *Owensboro Directory.*
Interview with Cris Hart, 2006.
Interview with Todd Reynolds, 2006.
Interview with Ann Welsh, 2006.
Interview with Belinda Thomson, 2005.
Investigation with P.A.S.T, Stan and Julie Howard, 2010.
Interview with Todd Reynolds, May 24, 2016.

Author David Wolfe was born in Coshocton, Ohio to Dave and Jan Rose Wolfe. At the age of 13, the family moved to Owensboro, Kentucky. David's parents divorced when he was young. His mother and he remained in their home and shortly thereafter, David began having paranormal experiences.

David's family have always been storytellers. His grandparents and his parents told him stories about ghosts, Bigfoot and other, fantastic tales. Little did they know, this fueled his love of history. David obtained a History Degree from Brescia University.

One of his biggest influences is local celebrity, Joe Ford. He first met Joe when he came to his school on Halloween telling spooky stories. Later, David would visit Joe at his museum and listen to tales of Owensboro's rich history.

David began his Haunted Ghost Tours of Owensboro and has been sharing his research and knowledge of Owensboro's spooky tales with thousands of patrons throughout the years.

His love of the paranormal and Owensboro has spawned this book and it is his hope that you enjoy these stories.

42524809R10086

Made in the USA
Middletown, DE
14 April 2017